# THE OFFICIAL

# SCRAPBOOK

# THE OFFICIAL

# SCRAPBOOK

## BY PETE ROSE

### Introduction by
### Hal McCoy

An Associated Features Book

A SIGNET SPECIAL
**NEW AMERICAN LIBRARY**
TIMES MIRROR

**IN THE SCRAPBOOK BULLPEN**

Editor: Zander Hollander/Associated Features
Writer: Hal McCoy/Dayton Daily News
Designer: Gerry Burstein/SoHo Studio


**PHOTO CREDITS**

Cover: Malcolm Emmons, Mickey Palmer/Focus on Sports, Rich Pilling, Carl Skalak.
George Gojkovich: 2, 28 (left), 51
Terry Armor (Cincinnati Enquirer): 6
UPI: 8, 17, 18, 19, 21, 23, 25, 26, 27, 29, 30, 31, 32, 33, 34, 35, 37, 40, 42, 43, 44, 46, 50, 52, 53, 54, 56 (bottom), 58, 59, 60, 61, 62, 63, 64, 65, 66, 67, 68 (top), 69, 70, 72, 73, 76, 77, 79, 81, 82, 83, 85, 86, 87, 88, 91, 93, 94, 97, 98, 108, 110, 111, 112, 113, 116, 122, 125
Pete Rose Collection: 11, 12, 13, 14, 117, 118
Cincinnati Reds: 15, 119
Jack Klumpe (Cincinnati Post): 16, 48, 55, 56 (top)
Ken Regan: 20
Wide World: 22, 45, 57, 95, 96, 114
Carl Skalak, Jr.: 24
Dennis Gruelle: 28 (bottom), 41, 68 (bottom), 120 (top), 121, 123, 124, 127 (top left)
Malcolm Emmons: 36, 75
Clifton Boutelle: 38
Frank Bryan: 39
Robert C. Bartosz: 47
Richard Pilling: 49
Ed Reinke (Cincinnati Enquirer): 100
Fred Straub (Cincinnati Enquirer): 84
Jeff Hinckley (Cincinnati Enquirer): 89
Ray Boeh: 109
ABC-TV: 115
Gerry Wolter (Cincinnati Enquirer): 120 (bottom)
Swanson: 126
Aqua Velva: 127 (top right)
Mountain Dew-PepsiCo, Inc.: 127 (bottom)

SIGNET, SIGNET CLASSICS, MENTOR, PLUME and MERIDIAN BOOKS
are published by The New American Library Inc., 1301 Avenue of the Americas,
New York, New York 10019.

First Printing Oct., 1978

1  2  3  4  5  6  7  8  9

PRINTED IN THE UNITED STATES OF AMERICA

To all those wonderful fans
all over the nation who rooted
for me and my streak
                    and

To the pitchers who made it possible.

                        Pete Rose

# CONTENTS

3 -K-
BRAVES

# INTRODUCTION

Atlanta's Gene Garber, wearing an evil looking beard, peered for a sign from catcher Joe Nolan. Peter Edward Rose, hunched over in that familiar deep crouch, waited patiently, his bat barely moving.

The scoreboard, in huge numbers, told the 31,159 fans in Atlanta-Fulton County Stadium the count—two balls, two strikes.

It was a night game, Aug. 1, 1978, and the stadium was rocking and rolling to the beat of, "Let's Go, Pete. Let's Go, Pete." There were two outs in the ninth and Rose was 0-for-3.

The night before, Rose had extended his hitting streak to 44 games, tying the National League record set by Wee Willie Keeler in 1897. A week earlier he had set the modern National League record by hitting in his 38th consecutive game.

But now his bid to move past Keeler in pursuit of Joe DiMaggio's monumental mark of 56 straight games dangled on the precipice. Garber, a side-wheeling right-hander who turns his back completely on the hitter during his windup, shook off one sign from Nolan.

Finally, he nodded an affirmative and Rose began a practice swing, but stopped and returned the bat to its cocked position.

Garber began his motion, turning his back so that Rose was staring at the huge "26" on Garber's back. The pitch was on its way…a changeup on the outside corner. Rose tried a weak swing, missing. Strike three. The streak was over.

Garber leaped in circles on the mound as Rose slowly walked toward the Cincinnati dugout, nervously wiping his bat's barrel with his hand.

It was gone. Rose's dream of obtaining the unobtainable was over. One of baseball's Big Three records, the DiMaggio streak, was still safe—the only one of the three that Pete was capable of reaching. He couldn't hit 61 home runs in a year like Roger Maris, or 60 like Babe Ruth. He couldn't hit 755 home runs like Hank Aaron or 714 like Ruth. But, he thought, he might hit in 56 straight games. Veteran reliever Garber—and rookie starter Larry McWilliams—had shattered Pete's dream.

Rose's singular epic had started six weeks earlier, but it really began on April 14, 1941, the day he was born in the Western Hills section of Cincinnati, a lower middle class neighborhood.

He was a skinny, scraggly kid who never left that neighborhood until he signed his first baseball contract. He was a mascot for his father's semi-pro football team and a batboy for his dad's sandlot baseball team.

By age nine, Pete was switch-hitting. His far-sighted father taught him to do it, insisting that his Knothole League coach use him as a switch-hitter.

Rose's American Legion coach was not so far-sighted, cutting him from the team, but by his freshman year at Cincinnati Western Hills High School, Pete was a 130-pound baseball and football player.

Teammate Eddie Brinkman had no trouble signing a baseball contract, but Pete's uncle, Buddy Bloebaum, a bird dog scout, practically begged the Reds to give Rose a chance. They did…and the rest is on-going history.

Now, as a 16-year member of the Cincinnati Reds, Rose is on his way to a head-first slide into the Hall of Fame in this, his 38th year of life—an age when most men think they're getting exercise when they climb out of an electric cart and stand long enough to swat a golf ball.

Rose, whose two favorite conversational topics are baseball and baseball, maintains he's not even thinking retirement.

"For sure, I'm not going nowhere until I catch Stan Musial," says the man on a search mission for Musial's 3,630 career hits, the all-time National League record. "Then my epitaph can be, 'Pete Rose: All he ever wanted was base hits. He wanted to hit forever.' "

Asked how he'd like to be remembered, Rose said, "It would be nice if they erected a statue of me in front of Riverfront Stadium like they did for Musial in front of Busch Stadium in St. Louis. If they did, at least it would keep the dogs happy and my friends could sleep under it. I don't want to be buried there, though."

That's vintage Rose. While giving you serious thoughts, he spices them with humor and sprinkles them with an endless stream of statistics. And he's seldom wrong.

His manager, Sparky Anderson, sums up Rose succinctly with, "He is willing to play every day, which is rare nowadays. There will never be another one like him. He's a street fighter who scratched and clawed for everything he got."

Age always has been meaningless to Rose, also known in his hometown as The Cincinnati Kid and Charlie Hustle. He is idolized in Redsland, which encompasses Southwestern Ohio, Northern Kentucky, Southeastern Indiana and Southwestern West Virginia. When you say Pete Rose, you've said Cincinnati Reds. And, when you've said Cincinnati Reds, you've said Pete Rose. Simple as that.

One of Pete's favorite expressions about age is, "I'm 37, going on 21."

As baseball writer for the Dayton Daily News, covering the Reds home and away for the past seven years, I've lived the summers with Pete Rose. I'm the same age as Pete and he makes me ashamed to complain about being tired or bored. Pete Rose is never tired, never bored with baseball.

Usually, he is first at the park, last to leave—living and talking the game with whomever will listen.

To those who don't know him, the casual fan, Pete Rose is a rough-around-the-edges, hell-bent-for-second-base ruffian, a pile of numbers as he sets record after record. He is more than that. He is a one-of-a-kind human being.

Pete Rose makes me feel like 37, going on 21.

**Hal McCoy**

# GROWING UP

I wonder whether I could have made it as a pro football player. Hey, I might have been a Cincinnati Bengal. I started early enough—as mascot for my father's semi-pro team.

I hadn't begun to switch-hit yet. Or it could be that I was facing left-handers when these pictures were taken.

We had a team called the Sedansville Civic Club that played in the
Cincinnati Knothole League. Can you pick me out? I'm the smallest one
in the back row, fourth from the left. There's another future major
leaguer in the front row, last one on the right. He's Eddie Brinkman,
who got to play his first big league game  with the Washington
Senators in 1961, two years before I did. Eddie was born the day after
Pearl Harbor, Dec. 8, 1941. Eddie was one heckuva fielder, and he's in
the record book, too. I hope he doesn't mind my pointing it out—fewest
hits in a season, 82, made with Washington in 1965.

The cover of the 1959 Western Hills High School Annual has these words as its theme: THE PRICELESS INGREDIENT... ENTHUSIASM. And inside there is a quotation by Ralph Waldo Emerson: "Nothing great was ever achieved without enthusiasm." I guess that's been my theme all along. The annual refers to me as a "shifty scatback" and that's me carrying the ball against Hughes High. We ended up as Public High School League co-champions for 1958 and one of the highlights for me was when I ran 68 yards for a touchdown against Walnut Hills. I think I was a better football player than a baseball player in high school. I was a starting back as a freshman. But in my sophomore year they kept the guy who played behind me the year before because he weighed 175 and I was only 130. That broke my heart, but I got to play the next year.

My class at Western Hills High. I'm in the top row, fifth from the right, and I don't need a haircut.

# THE ROOKIE

My second year in the minors—with the Tampa
Tarpons—I broke the club record for triples the first
month of the season and I had 30 of 'em for the year.
Look at my number... 11. I was No. 11 my first year
at Geneva (N.Y.), too. When I signed my first
contract in 1960, I cashed my bonus check at the
corner drugstore and took my first airplane ride. I
didn't have any luggage but I cured that. The fans
voted me Most Popular Player and I won a set of
luggage. My first year in the spring training with the
Reds (1963) I was No. 27 because I wasn't on the big
league roster. I got No. 14 the night before Opening
Day.

The two most influential men in my life, without question, were my dad and my first major league manager, Fred Hutchinson. My dad, on the left, was one hell of an athlete, playing semi-pro football right into his 40's. The reason I'm where I am right now is because he made sure I stayed a switch hitter. I'm probably one of the few kids ever to be a switch-hitter in a league at nine years old. Hutch—that's him on the right—always looked after me. He gave me my first job, and it wasn't a popular move because Don Blasingame, the second baseman I replaced, was very popular with the other players. But Hutch stayed with me. What a tough guy. He was dying of cancer in 1964, and knew it, but stayed with the team until the very end.

16

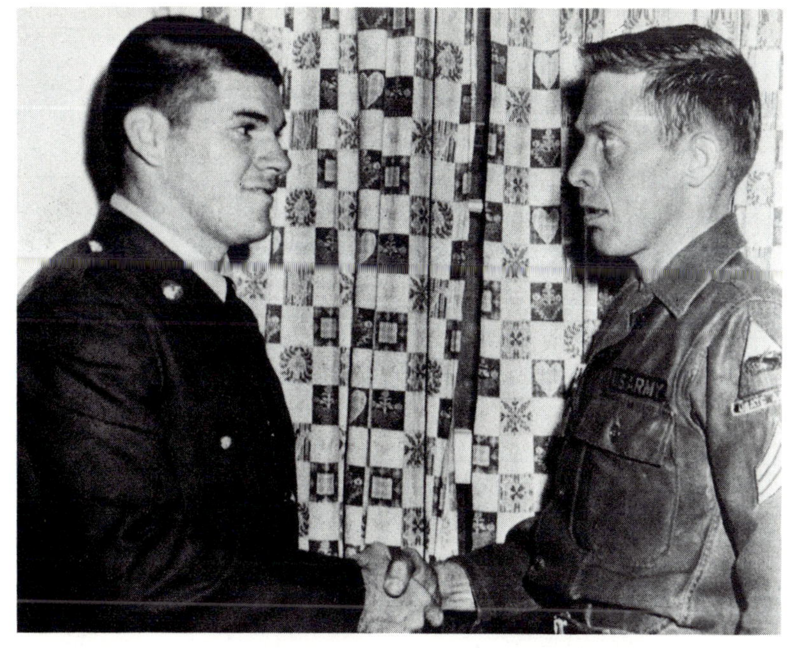

I was a weekend warrior for a while. When I went to basic training in November, 1963, I didn't even have to get a haircut. I always kept it as short as Army regulation anyway, until a few years ago. My platoon sergeant was Lester Axson. I got out of basic training in time for spring training in 1964, then served the rest of my time doing guard duty on weekends.

Gary Peters of the White Sox and I were Rookies of the Year together in 1963 and the Savannah Sugar Company gave us those huge trophies because we played against each other in the old Sally League when I played at Macon, Ga. I still have that trophy, my first real important one. I beat out New York's Ron Hunt for Rookie of the Year and the New York writers thought he should have won it. All he did was hit .260-something and he didn't deserve it. I had 170 hits.

# SECOND BASE WAS FIRST

18

I played second my first four years and I liked it because of a lot of involvement and I stayed in better shape there because I got so many ground balls and figured in double plays. They moved me to the outfield to make room for Tommy Helms. I never was a polished second baseman because I only started playing there when I was a sophomore at Western Hills High. That gave me four years of experience before I went to the big leagues. On the facing page, that's my ol' buddy, Milwaukee's Mack Jones (48), ducking under me at second in 1965. I'm kind of straddling Houston's Ron Brand on the opening half of a double play in another 1965 photo. In a 1967 game against the Braves, I've just got the force-out on Felipe Alou. But I'll remember that game because I hit two home runs.

# THE SWITCH-HITTER

My father told my knothole (Little League) coach if he'd give his word that I'd be a switch-hitter, always bat left-handed against right-handed pitchers and right-handed against left-handed pitchers, he'd never take me away for vacations during the season, his obligation to the ball club. Since I started doing it at nine, I don't know if I'm naturally left or right, but I do everything else right-handed. The advantage of switch-hitting is that the curve ball is always coming into you, but there is a disadvantage. Most switch-hitters aren't pull hitters, so that eliminates home runs, with the exception of Mickey Mantle. People don't realize it—that even with only 148 home runs, I'm the all-time leader in the National League. When I got my 2,881st hit in St. Louis (July 25, 1977) I passed Frankie Frisch as the No. 1 switch-hitter of all time. Not many guys in baseball or any sport become the all-time best at whatever they do. I couldn't become the best home run hitter or RBI man, but I worked a lot of hours on switch-hitting. The whole secret is not trying to be something you're not. You can tell from the uniform on the left that it's early Pete Rose. Above, I'm in the 1972 World Series.

21

# UP AGAINST THE WALL

In the one where I'm an acrobat, I almost caught that ball. There's a gate in Philadelphia on the foul line in left field and when I got on top of it, it swung open. Boy, I really ran into that son-of-a-gun. I really wanted to catch it because my little buddy Larry Bowa hit it. I always thought I was a good outfielder because of my infield play. Being an infielder helped you in the outfield because you knew how deep infielders could come back on popups and you knew exactly where they would locate for cutoffs and I super-charged the ball in the outfield because that's your first step as an infielder. You know, in almost 1,500 games in the outfield, I have the all-time fielding record and nobody knows that (.996). I had a couple years I didn't even make an error. The outfield is easier to play because there's less wear and tear on your body. As far as communication, there's a gap in the outfield. You can't chatter with people as I like to do.

ROSE
14

# HEAD FIRST

I never had good foot speed, but I think since I first came to the majors 16 years ago, I've been the best at going from first to third on a single or from home to second on a double. I always leave home thinking about an extra base. If I have a cinch double, I'm thinking of a triple. If I have a cinch single, I'm always thinking double. When I'm on first base, I'm always looking for the hit to go to third base, and I ALWAYS know the situation as far as outs and score of the game. What makes a base-runner is to know when to run, how the outfielders throw…even what the outfielder did the last inning. If the outfielder just got through striking out with the bases loaded he might be easier to run on that inning. That's why it helps you to get to know the personality of the other players. Some guys take a strikeout right out to the position with them and other guys don't. I even bunt on a lot of guys who just got finished striking out. Take advantage of everything, that's what this game is about.

You know, I can't remember when I first began sliding head first but I know why. The way I do it, you pick up momentum and get to the base faster and don't have to rely on a coach…because you can see the ball if it squirts by a fielder. I don't recommend doing it into home. Normally, I slide feet first into home unless the catcher is reaching to the first base side of home. Then, I can come in head first and slide away from his shin guards, and I don't like sliding into shin guards. You get spiked on your arm, it won't hurt as much as if you get spiked on your knee or your ankle.

It's a high throw to the Cardinals' Ted Simmons in 1973 and this time
I'm feet first.

I was in a rundown here against the Giants at Candlestick in 1974.
That's catcher Dave Rader and his leggings behind me. I was safe.

# CONVERSATION CORNER

They moved me back to the infield again, this time to make room for George Foster in left field in 1975. I worked hard at learning to play third base because I always want to play good at defense for a couple of reasons. It's an obligation to the pitcher not to just go out there and go through the motions. He's working his tail off to get hitters out so I want to work just as hard helping him. And, when you play with Gold Glovers like Joe Morgan and Johnny Bench and Dave Concepcion and Cesar Geronimo it's embarrassing to play bad defense. I want to do good defensively. Hitting is only one phase of the game and if you play defense when you're not hitting well, you still help the team.

Mostly, I merely chat with umpires. I probably talk more to umpires than any other player, particularly the third base umpire when I'm on defense. I am, though, miffed at plate umpire Bob Stewart in this picture. I claim I was hit with a pitch on the foot. Umpire Stewart said no. Guess who won? I'm 0-for-100 in disagreements with umpires. This one happened in the 1970 World Series against Baltimore. Umpires have a difficult job and you gotta give 'em credit. Instant replays show they are right far more often than wrong.

# ALL-STAR GAME

Ah, the infamous Ray Fosse wreck at home plate in the 1970 All-Star Game in Cincinnati. I scored the winning run from second on Jim Hickman's single in the 12th inning and we won, 5-4. Fosse had the plate blocked and I was fortunate to get there before the ball. Fosse was at my house the night before until three in the morning and I had bought him dinner. So, I was really concerned how he was after the play. I bent over and asked if he was all right, even though my knee was hurting. I missed three games after that, but Fosse played the rest of Cleveland's season with a shoulder separation. It didn't show up on the X-rays. He was reaching for the ball just as I got to the plate and you can see where the plate is, behind his foot. I wanted to slide head first, but I couldn't make it. I tagged home plate with my right hand.

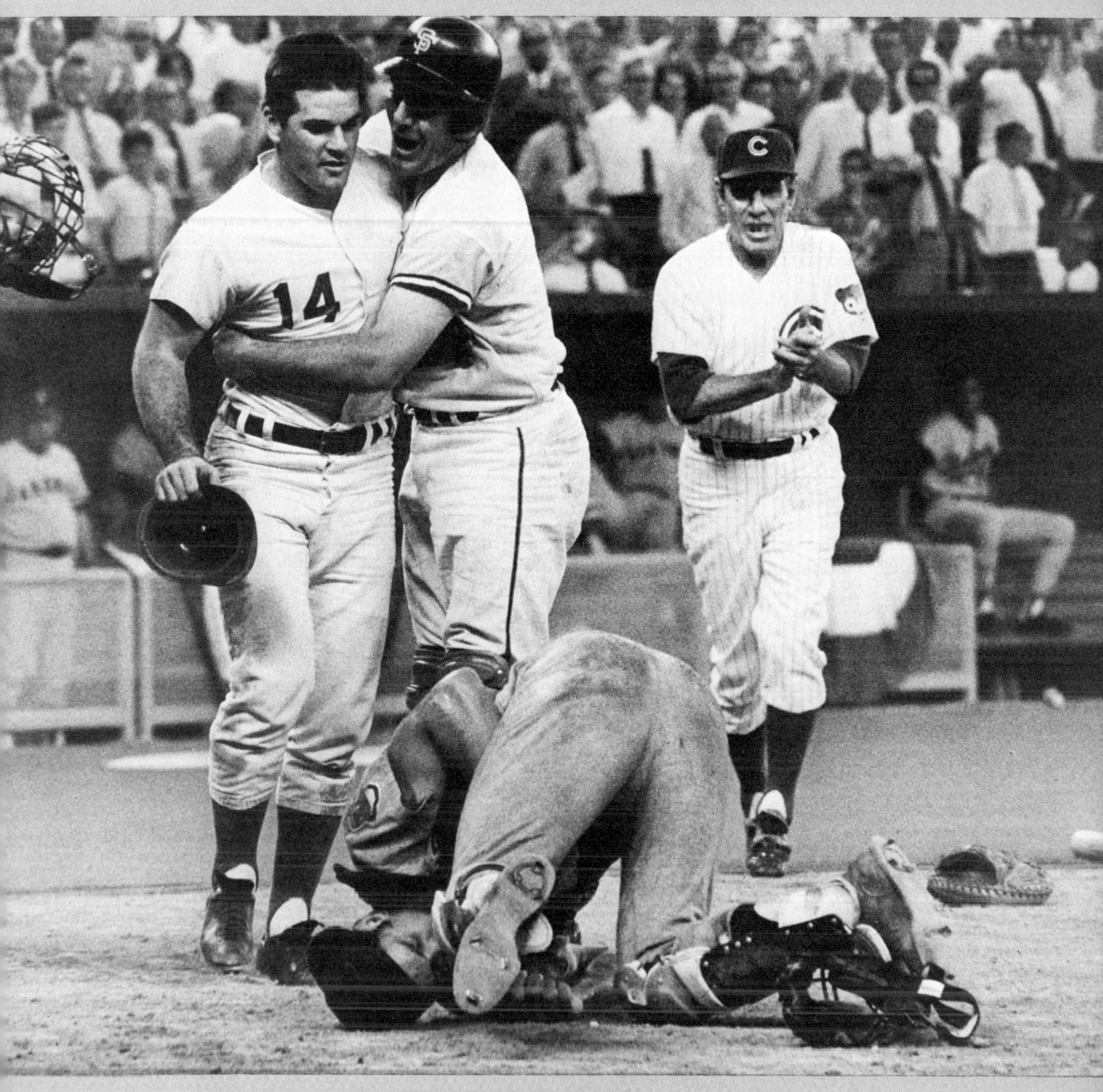

The Giants' Dick Dietz is congratulating me and Leo Durocher, who was the Cubs' manager then, is applauding, too. At that moment I was obviously shook up myself.

I was fortunate enough in 1973 to play in the All-Star Game in Kansas City with a couple of great outfielders, the premier center fielder of just before my time, Willie Mays, and the best all-around center fielder now, Houston's Cesar Cedeno. Mays and Cedeno are similar; both could do it all. I've seen pictures of Willie's 1954 World Series catch off Vic Wertz and it's the best I've ever seen.

I'm often asked if I hate pitchers. No, I don't. I love 'em. They've made me a pretty good living. I'm sure pitchers in the National League respect me, just as I'm sure pitchers in the American League respect Rod Carew. That's Rod sliding into me at third base in the 1978 All-Star Game in San Diego after leading off the game with a triple. Need I say the man can hit?

# THE MANY FACES OF *Pete Rose*

34

That son-of-a-gun hurt, even though it was a Phil Niekro
knuckleball. I didn't rub it, though. Can't give a pitcher the
satisfaction of knowing that it stings. A writer asked me to
compare Niekro's fast ball to another pitcher's and I told him
I'd rather not do that. But I did tell him that after watching
Niekro's knuckler, his fast ball comes in there like Herb
Score's, or if you're from a younger generation, Sandy
Koufax's. I've had some hits off Phil. The toughest guys for me
have been Jim Brewer and Randy Jones. They're the only left-
handed pitchers off whom I tried to bat left-handed. That
didn't work, either.

I can't sit down much in the dugout. When we're hitting and even when I'm out of the game sometimes in late innings, I don't sit. I'm up on the front rail watching, for a couple of reasons. I like to watch the game, of course...keeping totally involved. And, I like to listen to manager Sparky Anderson because he's usually standing right there close to me. By standing, rather than sitting, I feel it's easier to keep posted on the game. If I'm going to manage some day, I have to put myself in the manager's place and that's what I do in the dugout.

I hate to face a pitcher for the first time. I like to know exactly what a pitcher throws and how he throws 'em. That's why I don't usually do well against a pitcher the first time I face him. If I don't know him, I study him intently as he warms up. You watch what he throws, how he releases the ball, which way he twists his wrist for breaking pitches. You look for screwballs and forkballs—the trick pitches. When Larry McWilliams stopped my 44-game hitting streak, I'd never faced him. They said he threw a forkball and I kept looking for it, but I never saw it.

Batting practice is not just a show for early-arriving fans. I try to
do in batting practice exactly the same thing I'll do in a game.
Try to get the ball out in front, hit the ball hard to all fields…and
usually it works. That's what batting practice is for, practice.
And, to do a little kibitzing with members of the other team. I get
up there at the end of batting practice and try to jerk balls out of
the park, if I've had enough practice strokes on my base hits.
Too many guys don't use batting practice in the right way. Try to
play long ball, hit all home runs. I find that if I hit well in batting
practice, I hit well in games.

# BATTING PRACTICE

Although I may seem to have a pained expression on my face, I'm not in pain. I'm just relaxing after some batting practice. And even if I had pain, I'd play. You have to play with some pain. Anybody can play when everything is going good. I've always been fortunate to stay away from leg injuries and my arms are big, so I don't have any arm injuries. Stomach pulls and stuff like that, I always wonder how guys get that, I've never had anything like that. I guess that's why I was able to play in 678 straight games right up to the time I was 36 years old.

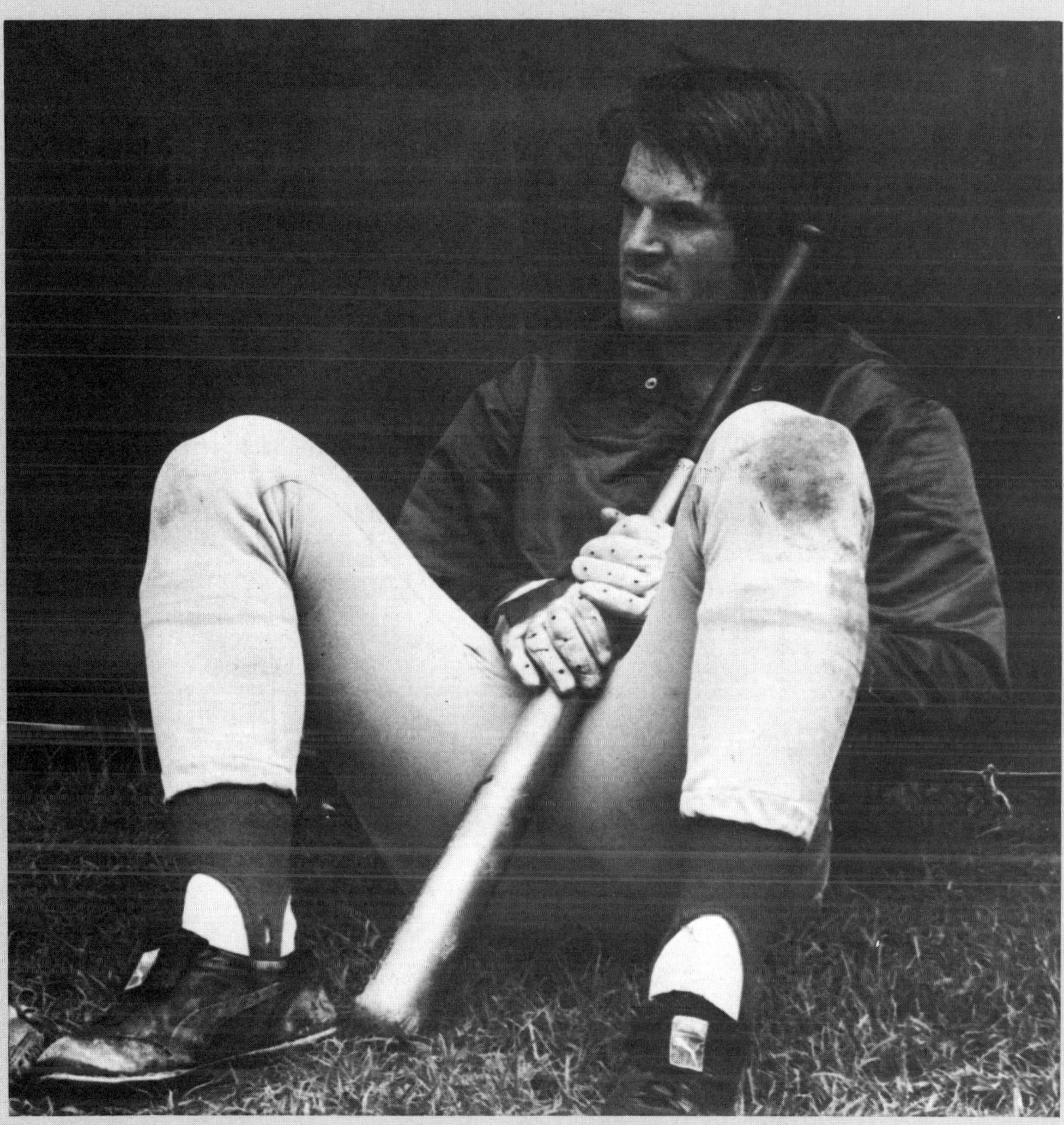

# THE HARRELSON

I was playing like I always play, hard, not dirty. I tried to break up a double play in the 1973 Playoffs with the Mets and nearly started World War III. I knocked the Mideast war off the front pages of the New York newspapers. Bud Harrelson and I had a little wrestling match and everything was cool until the benches emptied and Wayne Garrett and Jerry Koosman punched me in the back. Big Ted Kluszewski and Johnny Bench wrestled me away. All I ever did was grab Harrelson and throw him down because I thought he was going to swing at me.

# INCIDENT

The fans got so vicious, throwing bottles and stuff, that the first time we went back to Shea Stadium the next season, they didn't sell any tickets in left field. There was really no animosity between Bud and me and we appeared at a luncheon together a couple of days later to show the people we were still friends. I know, and Harrelson knows, if the situation arose again, I'd go into him just as hard. It's the way I play baseball.

# TEAMMATES AND FRIENDLY FOES

Johnny Bench is a tremendous, tremendous catcher. I didn't see any of the real old-timers but it would be difficult for me to believe there has ever been a better defensive catcher or a better all-around catcher. I sort of took him under my wing when he first came up, as I try to do with all young players. Blocking the plate, making the tag—he's unbelievable. He has such big hands—he can hold seven baseballs in one hand—he is one of the very few one-handed catchers I've seen using that flexible glove.

That's Pee Wee Bowa watching me swing the bat. He sure looks
scraggly here. Looks like my son. He's filled out now working on the
Nautilus equipment. I consider Bowa and Greg Luzinski, both of the
Phillies, two of my best buddies in baseball. When they come to town, I
take 'em home with me to eat. Now, Bowa is a guy who has really made
himself into a good, solid baseball player. He worked at it, overcame a
lot of things. Mike Schmidt said it's because of me and maybe it is
because I never stopped harping at him. We're a lot alike in a lot of
ways.

After the 1965 season, Cincinnati owner Bill DeWitt sold super-popular
Frank Robinson to the Baltimore Orioles, after Frank played 10 years
with the Reds. Somebody asked DeWitt why he sold Robby when he
was only 31 and Bill said, "Because he's an old 31." I wonder if Mr.
DeWitt would think I'm an old 37. I think I'm a young 21, myself. We're
in spring training in Tampa in this picture before the 1966 season and
that's Tommy Harper with me and Robby.

I never thought Tom Seaver had much of a sense of humor when he
pitched for the New York Mets. I just knew he was one helluva pitcher.
I discovered when he joined us in mid-June of 1977 that he was quite
loose, a lot of fun. The guy is smart, intelligent, competitive and he's
always thinking on the mound. Now, a lot of pitchers have those
ingredients, but Seaver mixes in a lot of talking to himself and to the
defensive players. He even has fun while he pitches, but it's not much
fun for the hitters.

There's The Hammer. I know writers didn't believe me, but all through my 44-game batting streak when I was chasing Joe DiMaggio's record 56-game streak, I kept saying that some day somebody would get DiMaggio's record. The one record I think will stand forever is Hank Aaron's career 755 homers. Nobody will come close. Players won't play the game long enough. I always liked Hank because he found time to say hi to you. We didn't have anything in common as far as hitting home runs, but we chatted baseball a lot. People in Atlanta liked it when I said what better place to end the streak at 44 than in Atlanta, the number The Hammer wore.

50

Joe Morgan is my next-door neighbor in the clubhouse. When he wants to talk about something I listen. When I want to talk about something, he listens. We've been pals for so long that I came up with a name for us a couple of years ago, Salt and Pepper. Joe is the clubhouse needler, the guy who keeps everybody loose with meaningful barbs. It amazes me to listen to Joe talking to writers. Ask him one question and you get a five-minute answer. And it all makes sense.

I won my second batting title in 1969 and National League Secretary Fred Fleig visited Riverfront Stadium in 1970 to present me with a plaque and The Silver Bat. I've come a long way since hitting .273 and .269 my first two years—even if I did win Rookie of the Year. If I hit .269 now, I'd be jumping off the Tallahatchee Bridge.

# THE HIT PARADE

Good Ol' President Emeritus Warren Giles of the National League
presents me with my 1973 Most Valuable Player plaque. That was really
nice, something special. It took a long time to win that. I won the batting
title with .338, leading the league with 230 hits, my all-time high. It's one
of my proudest achievements because it's tough for a guy who doesn't
hit a lot of home runs and drive in a lot of runs. You gotta do a lot of
other things—like win the batting title.

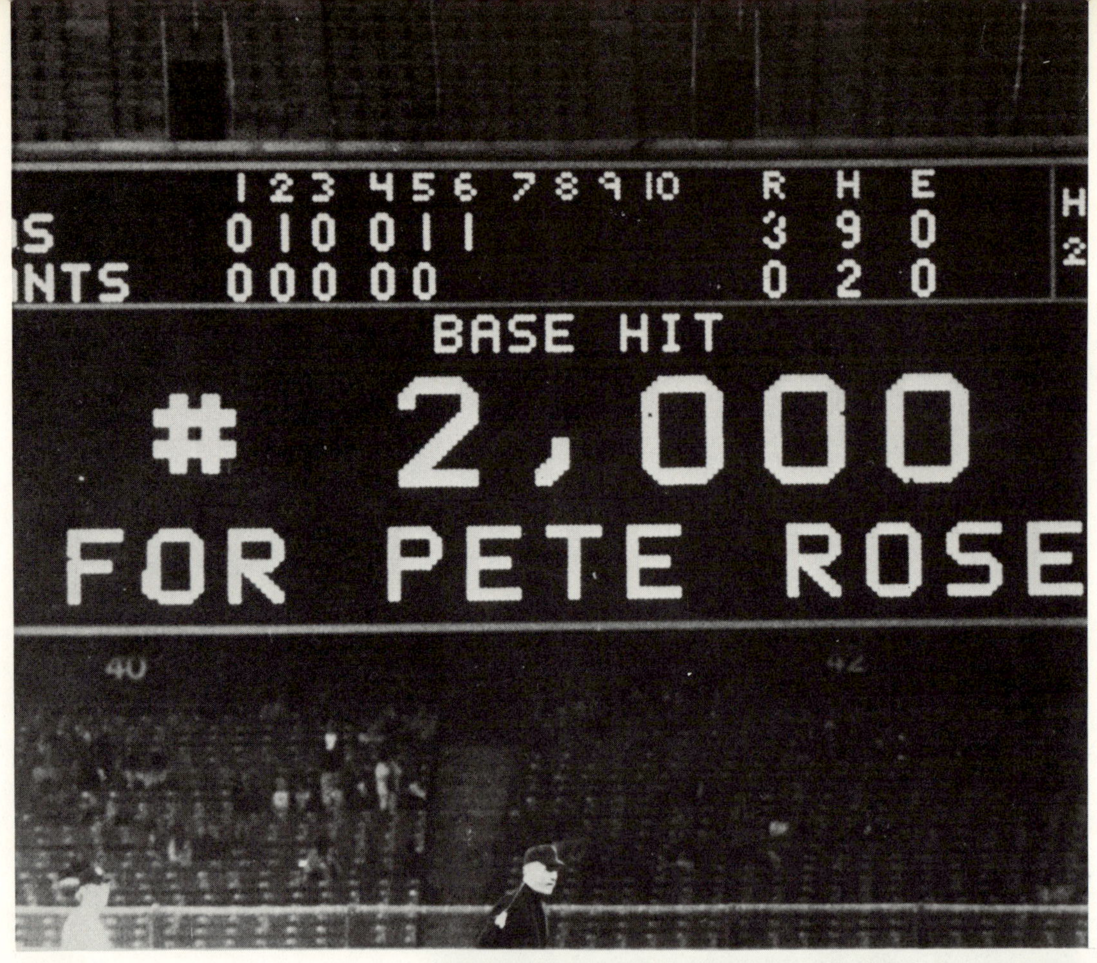

I've doffed my cap so often the past couple of years I'm losing my hair. This one is for career hit No. 2,000, achieved in the sixth inning of the June 20, 1973 game in San Francisco's Candlestick Park. King Kong Kingman is with me at first base. When he hits 'em, he doesn't stop at first. He circles the bases. We won that game, by the way, 4-0.

54

No. 2,500 came in 1975 when I singled off Pittsburgh's Bruce Kison at Riverfront Stadium. I ended the season with 2,547 hits, second to Lou Brock among then active National Leaguers.

I agreed 100 percent with those fans sitting in Riverfront Stadium—I wanted my 3,000th hit, too. I knew what they meant, though. Most of my milestone hits have been on the road and I really wanted to get this one before the home fans. Fortunately, that's what happened. I made it off Montreal's Steve Rogers on May 5, 1978. As I went along, writers asked me if I felt pressure going after 3,000. Heck, no. I started 1978 needing 34 hits to make it and I knew I could go at least 34-for-600 in 1978.

One thing right off the top. I am not crying here. Big boys don't cry, do they? I'm just wiping the sweat off my eyes, or something. No tears, though. I was happy enough to cry, but I didn't. It was my 3,000th hit and that's my good friend, Tony Perez of the Montreal Expos, behind me. I was glad he got to see it. I laughed when I heard what Johnny Bench said about me. They asked him what he'd be doing when he was 50 and he said he'd be in the stands watching me play third base.

# WHAT IT'S ALL ABOUT: PLAYOFFS AND WORLD SERIES

The tractor is the Original Big Red Machine, born in 1970. I've read
where some sportswriter is credited with coming up with that name for
the Cincinnati Reds. Uh, uh. Manager Dave Bristol and I came up with
that name. We were the first to call the Reds The Big Red Machine.
There are some pretty good players sitting there—Bobby Tolan,
Johnny Bench, Tony Perez, Lee May and myself. It just seemed like in
1970 we played like a machine, you know? We got it together and rolled
over everybody, winning a lot of games by 8-10 runs. We won 70 of our
first 100.

That's my best friend in baseball, Doggie—Tony Perez. I guess
that shows it all when you start spitting champagne instead of
drinking it. This is after we beat Atlanta in mid-September of
1970 to clinch the Western Division title. I think I put out
Doggie's cigar with that stream I'm firing at him. That's always
fun when you celebrate with the champagne by pouring it on
everybody's head and squirting it in their faces. It's sort of
symbolic of what the whole season is about and the
champagne signifies your reward.

Even though we were down two games to none to Baltimore in the 1970 World Series, there was time for some horseplay. Pitcher Milt Wilcox is my mount and pinch-hitter Angel Bravo is watching. Bravo came up with one of the all-time funny lines that season. Known as a pinch-hitter, Bravo had to play in a few games and he told manager Dave Bristol, "Bench me or trade me." That 1970 Series belonged to Baltimore third baseman Brooks Robinson. He robbed us of base hits so many times down there we thought we were hitting against the Berlin Wall. This photo illustrates, though, even when your back is against the wall, it's best to try to stay loose. The world isn't going to end if you don't win. It just seems that way at the time. The Orioles won in five.

I had a bunch of hits in the 1972 National League Playoffs against the Pirates but Johnny Bench was our big hero with one of the most dramatic home runs I've ever seen. We lost the first game, 5-1, but won the second game, 5-3. The Pirates won the next one, 3-2, then Ross Grimsley pitched a two-hitter and we evened it up, two games each. Roberto Clemente got both hits off Grimsley and who would have guessed the next game would be Clemente's last one before dying in that tragic plane crash? What a loss to baseball. I really respected that man. The Pirates led, 3-2, going into the bottom of the ninth of the final game. Bench fouled off a bunch of pitches against Dave Giusti, then lined a homer over the right field fence. Then, with two outs, George Foster scored from third base on a Bob Moose wild pitch to give us the pennant. Some game. Some champagne.

I'd walk through hell in a gasoline suit for Sparky Anderson. I think that much of him. Sparky is good because he treats a man like a man and a boy like a boy. He's always treated me that way. If you had a personal problem, you could go to Sparky and he'd try to help you out. Sparky and I are checking out the Oakland Coliseum for the 1972 World Series. It was the first time either of us saw it. Look at those clothes we have on! Sparky's come a long way, and sprouted more grey hair.

The 1972 World Series was one of the closest in history, they tell me.
Six of the seven games were decided by one run and the Oakland A's
beat us, 3-2, in the final game with Gene Tenace catching my line drive
against the wall to end it. I remember hitting a home run on the first
pitch of Game Five. Mostly I remember how I hit Catfish Hunter. I got
most of my hits off him after making one of my "famous" statements. I
said he was a good pitcher, but not a great one. He was offended by it.
Our Ed Sprague was a good friend of his and I told Ed to tell him I was
gonna hit him, and on that first pitch of the game I did. I'm not hitting it
here. Ken Holtzman is throwing the first pitch of Game Four. It was a
strike.

In Game Six, the A's are giving me an intentional pass, and they are really giving me one, which is probably why I'm laughing as catcher Gene Tenace signals for the wide pitches. Earlier in the game, with a 3-and-2 count, the A's pulled off that trick where they acted as if they were giving Johnny Bench an intentional walk but struck him out instead. I don't think there are too many guys, even if they were alert, who would have hit that pitch. The pitch was right on the outside corner, and thrown hard. I won't ever criticize John for getting caught napping, because that was some kind of pitch.

There are some pretty well-known sportswriters gathered around me here in New York during the 1973 Playoffs. That's Milt Richman of United Press International in the foreground. Si Burick of the Dayton Daily News and the late Arthur Daley of the New York Times are behind Milt, with Pat Harmon of the Cincinnati Post over my left shoulder. I've always tried to cooperate with reporters because I realize they have a job to do, and a very important job as far as ballplayers are concerned. Too many of us don't realize that and if ballplayers and writers get along together, we're all better off. Actually, it's my job to cooperate with writers. ►

When you see me on the on-deck circle rubbing my bat with a rag, I'm putting pine tar on the handle. It's a sticky substance to make your hands and bat stick together. I put it on my bats before every at-bat, but the next day before a game I take some alcohol and rub if all off. I don't want it to cake up on my bat. I can't hit without it, though. It's a comfort. Hitting without pine tar is like me hitting with too heavy a bat. I use a 33½-ounce, 35-inch R195 bat. I'm preparing here for the 1975 Playoffs against Pittsburgh. I guess the tar helped. We beat the Pirates three straight and I got a home run in the third game—as did Dave Concepcion—against John Candelaria.

For some reason, I don't remember this picture. But I'll always
remember that Carl Yastrzemski is a great ball player. The picture was
taken at Fenway Park sometime during the World Series of 1975. I
guess I got a little publicity for a comment I made after Game Six. Even
though we lost, to even the Series three to three, on Carlton Fisk's 12th-
inning homer, I told everybody I saw, "Wasn't that the greatest sporting
event you ever saw? There couldn't have been any Super Bowl that
topped that game." It was the greatest game I ever saw, let alone played
in. Then, in Game Seven, I got what I call the most meaningful hit of my
career, and it isn't even listed among my 3,100-plus hits. We were
behind, 3-0, in the sixth until Tony Perez hit a homer to make it 3-2. I
singled home the tying run in the seventh and in the ninth, with two
outs and two strikes, Joe Morgan singled in the game-winner. What a
Series! I'm proud to say I was MVP of what some call the greatest
World Series ever. Well, that's what the writers who were there say.
And, I won't argue it.

Former Houston and Los Angeles outfielder Jimmy Wynn used to be known as The Toy Cannon, but that's no toy I'm messing with. It's the real thing, an antique cannon in the lobby of our hotel in Boston during the 1975 World Series. Check out my bow tie. The cannon pose gave me something to do when we were rained out.

The World's Greatest Manager and The World's Greatest Catcher—Sparky Anderson and Johnny Bench. If you think I'm prejudiced, well, tough. That's the way I feel. Bench is planting a kiss on Sparky's forehead after we won the 1975 World Series. Now, I like Sparky, but kiss him? Never.

Just call me Yogi Rose. That's what Johnny Bench called me, saying I looked like a young Yogi Berra when I appeared on Cincinnati's Fountain Square for a public celebration after we swept the Yankees four straight in the 1976 World Series. I'm giving the thumbs down to the Yankees, but I don't hate 'em. I just dislike 'em. But then, I dislike all teams not wearing red hats with a white "C."

# THE STREAK

What "The Streak" was all about, chasing The Yankee Clipper, Joltin' Joe DiMaggio.

On June 13, 1978, the Cincinnati Reds were shut out in Riverfront Stadium by the Chicago Cubs' Dennis Lamp, 1-0, on four hits.

Peter Edward Rose did not get one of those four hits. He was 0-for-3 with a walk.

In fact, after that game, Rose was 6-for-51 and his batting average was an uncharacteristic .269. "I'm not worried, though. I've been hitting the ball hard, but it's not finding the holes," Rose said.

The next day, June 14, with 37,749 sitting in Riverfront Stadium, Pete Rose lined two singles off Dave Roberts of the Cubs. And, Pete Rose kept hitting.

By the All-Star break, July 8, Rose had hit in 25 straight games, tying his own personal high. His only narrow escape was against Houston knuckleballer Joe Niekro in Game 21 of the streak. Rose was 0-for-3 in the eighth, but sent 32,647 Riverfront fans into a frenzy by dumping a perfect bunt in front of the plate and beating catcher Luis Pujols' peg.

"I really wanted to have a 25-game streak for the All-Star Game," Rose said. "That'd give 'em something nice to talk about on TV. Not even Howard Cosell could screw that up."

In the All-Star Game, Rose banged a hit off Cleveland's Jim Kern and said, "They ought to count that hit in my streak. Whenever I get a hit off a hard thrower like Kern, I'd like to have it count for something."

After the break, Rose resumed his onslaught of base hits. His first of an endless series of standing ovations came in Riverfront on July 14 when he singled off New York's Pat Zachry, a former Cincinnati teammate. The third-inning single tied him with former teammate Vada Pinson and old-timer Edd Roush for the modern Cincinnati club record, 27.

"When I played for the Reds, Pete's wife used to watch my German shepherd while we were on the road until the dog got hair on his Rolls Royce," said Zachry.

Rose claimed the team record the next day, 28, with a first-inning single off Craig Swan. Ex-St. Louis Cardinal player and manager Red Schoendienst was obliterated from the books as the top streaking switch-hitter when Rose reached 30 on July 17, a fifth-inning single off another ex-teammate, Montreal's Ross Grimsley.

The 30th game also tied him for the all-time club record, made by an obscure fellow somebody dredged from the depths during Pete's streak, Elmer Smith, 1898. Some other illustrious names were at 30—Stan Musial, Goose Goslin, Ron LeFlore. Musial is the man Rose is chasing for the all-time National League hits record, 3,630. Goslin and LeFlore had their streaks with the Detroit Tigers 42 years apart, 1934 and 1976.

Stan (The Man) Musial is the guy I'm really pursuing. During my streak, I passed him when I reached 31. Musial had 30 for the St. Louis Cardinals in 1950. But, it's his all-time National League total hits record I'm after, 3,630. A couple more good years and I'll get him. Ty Cobb's 4,191 is out of reach for the all-time baseball record. One of the greatest things to happen to me was in my rookie year when Musial was retiring and they gave him a day at old Busch Stadium. Manager Fred Hutchinson had me stand right at home plate near Musial when they lined both teams up along the base lines. "I want you to see this up close," Hutch told me. "That can be you some day." I never forgot that.

Until I came along, Ron LeFlore of the Detroit Tigers had the longest streak, 30 games, in six years. I give the guy a lot of credit for overcoming his life in prison and making it outside.

Of all the guys I passed during my streak, the name Goose Goslin intrigued me the most. He hit in 30 straight for the 1934 Detroit Tigers. Looking at his nose in this picture, I can see where he picked up the nickname Goose.

Now, the baseball world was awakening to Rose. Las Vegas put out odds, 1,000-to-1 that Rose wouldn't pass Joe DiMaggio's all-time 56-game record and 5-to-1 that Rose wouldn't pass the modern National League record, 37, by Tommy Holmes of the 1945 Boston Braves.

After the odds came out, there were some strange believers in Rose. Pete received a telegram with a three-word message, "Go, Go, Go" signed by Baccarat Dealers, Frontier Hotel, Las Vegas. They took the 5-to-1 odds.

Now, even fans in enemy ball parks pulled for Pete. Standing ovations met his every appearance and they chanted, "Pete, Pete, Pete." It continued in Montreal and New York after a stop in Philadelphia.

"The only time I thought I'd ever receive a standing ovation in Philly and New York was if I had a heart attack and died at third base," said Rose.

Suspense reached near the limit July 19 in Philadelphia. Tug McGraw walked Rose in the eighth inning, when he was 0-for-3. The 45,608 fans in Veterans Stadium booed McGraw, normally a local hero. But George Foster hit a grand slam homer and when Johnny Bench singled, Rose became assured of one more chance in the ninth to extend his streak to 32.

Ron Reed was the pitcher and he struck out Dan Driessen and Doug Bair. Once again, Rose was given an on-the-feet reception by the fans, and the Pete chant. On the first pitch, Rose dumped a bunt directly down the third-base line. Mike Schmidt charged, tried to make a bare-handed grab and throw in one motion, but missed. Rose was on, and the streak was still on—32.

That pushed Pete past four more all-time streakers who had 31—Sam Rice (1924), Willie Davis (1969), Fred Clarke (1895) and Rico Carty (1970).

"That's what happens when you play for a great offensive team like the Reds," Rose said. "I really thought the streak was over when I walked in the eighth, but Foster's slam gave me another shot. Ron Reed acted as if he was mad when I bunted in the ninth with a five-run lead (7-2). Normally, I wouldn't bunt with a five-run lead, but it took me 16 years to get to 31 in a row. If Schmidt gives me the bunt, I'll take it."

Philadelphia's Larry Bowa supported Rose.

"Pete Rose has never done anything bush in his life," Bowa said. "He's after a record everybody said would never be broken. All the rules are out the window. I expect Pete to try anything to get a hit."

The Reds moved to Montreal on July 21 and media interest perked up. Writers from Philadelphia and New York began following Rose's daily pursuit.

They didn't have to wait long for Rose to make their visits worthwhile. On Ross Grimsley's first pitch, Rose nearly shaved Grimsley's long, curly locks with a sizzler through the box—No. 34, pushing him past Heinie Manush, Rogers Hornsby and an ancient fellow named George Davis, all of whom were 33 streakers.

Willie Davis, a man who used his legs for hits to go along with a classic swing, went on a 31-game streak for the Dodgers in 1969. Willie was one of baseball's better outfielders, too.

Rico Carty is still around, taking advantage of his excellent hitting talents in the American League as a designated hitter. I passed him when I reached 32. Rico went on his 31-game streak in 1970 with Atlanta. Until my streak, Rico's was the longest in eight years.

**Another of the legends I've heard about through the years and whose name came up during my streak is Rogers Hornsby. I like his stylish swing. I guess that's why he hit in 33 straight games for the Cardinals in 1922 and hit over .400 three times, including an incredible .424 in 1924. Nobody will hit .400 in modern times. Relief pitchers are too good. You're always looking at a fresh arm.**

No. 35 and No. 36 came in Montreal off rookie pitcher Dan Schatzeder and All-Star pitcher Steve Rogers, the same guy off whom Rose lined his 3,000th hit in Riverfront May 5. The 35th game took Rose past some more notables, 34 streakers Dom DiMaggio (1949), George Sisler (1925), George McQuinn (1938) and John Stone (1930).

Before facing Schatzeder, Rose walked up to him and said, "Kid, how in hell am I supposed to get a hit off you when I can't even pronounce your name?" But he did, a single to center his fourth time up in the seventh, stretching the streak to 35, tying Ty Cobb's second longest streak (1917).

One thing Rose feared during the streak was facing a rookie pitcher for the first time. A scientific hitter, Rose likes to face a pitcher a couple of times to learn his style and his pitches.

Pete's sixth-inning single off Rogers in Game 36 tied him on the all-time list with Hall-of-Famer Bill Hamilton (1894).

So, it was on to New York—an appropriate spot for two reasons. Tommy Holmes, the National League record holder at 37, worked as Community Relations Director for the Mets, and would be in Shea Stadium. And, the media coverage reached near saturation. Besides the heavy-hitting New York press, there were journalists from Washington, Atlanta, Detroit, Boston, Philadelphia, Cleveland, Louisville, Montreal, Baltimore and the Reds' beat regulars from Cincinnati and Dayton.

Monday night's game was not the prime ABC-TV game, but the network cut in each time Rose batted to show the nation. Rose was mobbed by the media before the game and he was to set a standard, an unbelievable standard, right to the streak's end. He accommodated the press, radio and TV at every turn, talking as he dressed, sitting in the dugout to chat some more. And, they kept asking about pressure…pressure, pressure, pressure.

**Ted Williams of the Red Sox is recognized as one of the all-time best hitters, and he hit .406 in 1941, the year Joe DiMaggio put together his 56-game streak. Even Williams admitted that what DiMaggio did was one of the all-time great hitting feats and may not ever be matched. The fellow with the glasses, talking to Ted, is Joe DiMaggio's brother, Dom, who hit in 34 straight games in 1949. When I passed him, he sent me a telegram, urging me on.**

"Pressure? What pressure?" Rose asked. "This isn't pressure, it's fun. I don't consider talking to you guys as interviews. It's conversation about baseball. I ain't losin' no sleep, because I ain't sleeping with any of you sportswriters. I know you guys have jobs to do. I'm happy to help. I'll talk all night to anybody who wants to talk baseball." And he talked and he talked and he talked. The media gobbled every phrase—and Rose came up with something new and printable every night.

Holmes, affable and courteous, thanked Rose "for helping me relive my streak and for making me famous again when everybody had forgotten me. I'm pulling for him, living and dying with each pitch."

Rose was 0-for-3 against Pat Zachry when he stepped to the plate in the seventh. He listened as the Shea fans—many of the same folks who verbally crucified him after his scuffle at second base with Bud Harrelson in the 1973 playoffs, some hurling bottles at him—chanted, "Let's Go Pete." At 9:52 on the scoreboard clock, on the first pitch, Rose lined a single to left, tying Holmes at 37. The standing ovation lasted three minutes and Rose doffed his batting helmet, causing him to say later, "I've been tipping my cap so often I'm losing my hair."

Pete Rose posters and hand-painted signs covered Shea the next night, July 25, as Rose set out to pass Holmes. In the third inning, Rose drove a 1-and-1 Craig Swan pitch to left and the record was his. Holmes sprinted from his home plate seat to first base, retrieved the ball and presented it to Pete.

"I don't mind giving up a hit to Rose like that, he hit my best pitch," said Swan. "I tried to get him out, but I'm proud to be taken for an important base hit by one of the greatest players I've ever seen."

Rose tossed plaudits at Holmes, saying, "When somebody comes along and breaks my records, I hope I show as much class as this man has."

Pete's next goal was fifth spot on the all-time list, Ty Cobb's 40-game streak. "I'm glad there are people between me and Joe DiMaggio's 56-game record. I need immediate goals to drive me, that's what spurs me on.

"I never try to compare myself to Ty Cobb," Rose said. "But we do have three things in common. We would both do anything to win, we both hated to lose, and we've both got nine 200-hit seasons."

Rose closed his smash-hit New York appearance on July 26 with a third-inning line drive to right off Nino Espinosa to make it 39, then returned to Cincinnati to meet the Phillies in a Friday night doubleheader in front of 51,779 home fans. In the first game, Rose doubled to left in the third off Randy Lerch, running the streak to 40, tying Ty. In the second game, once again Rose resorted to the bunt, again pushing one Schmidt's way in the sixth when he was 0-for-2. Again Schmidt bobbled the ball trying to bare-hand it and Ty Cobb was history—and hello George Sisler's 41-game streak.

Although Tommy Holmes worked in 1978 for the New York Mets as Community Relations Director, I probably wouldn't have met him if I hadn't made the run for his 37-game National League record streak. That's Tommy in between Boston Brave pitchers Jim Tobin (left) and Mort Cooper after he beat Rogers Hornsby's record 33 in 1945.

# The Cincinnati Post

Tuesday evening, July 25, 1978

# Rose does it

## 37 down—immortality to go for hustling third baseman

Before this at-bat was the first time I noticed the chant, "Let's Go, Pete; Let's Go Pete." From 40,065 New York fans, no less. I guess those fans who threw things at me in the 1973 Playoffs retired from baseball. Anyway, it was the seventh inning and I was 0-for-3 trying to tie the National League record of 37. I stepped in against old friend Pat Zachry, who visited my house often when he was with the Reds. I faked a bunt, drawing third baseman Lenny Randle in, then punched the hit past him...No. 37. Three hitters later, Zachry was taken out and kicked the dugout step so hard he fractured a toe. Same old Zach. A writer asked me about being nervous about setting the record of 38 and I said, "The only thing I'm worried about is catching the team bus tonight." I meant it. But I missed it.

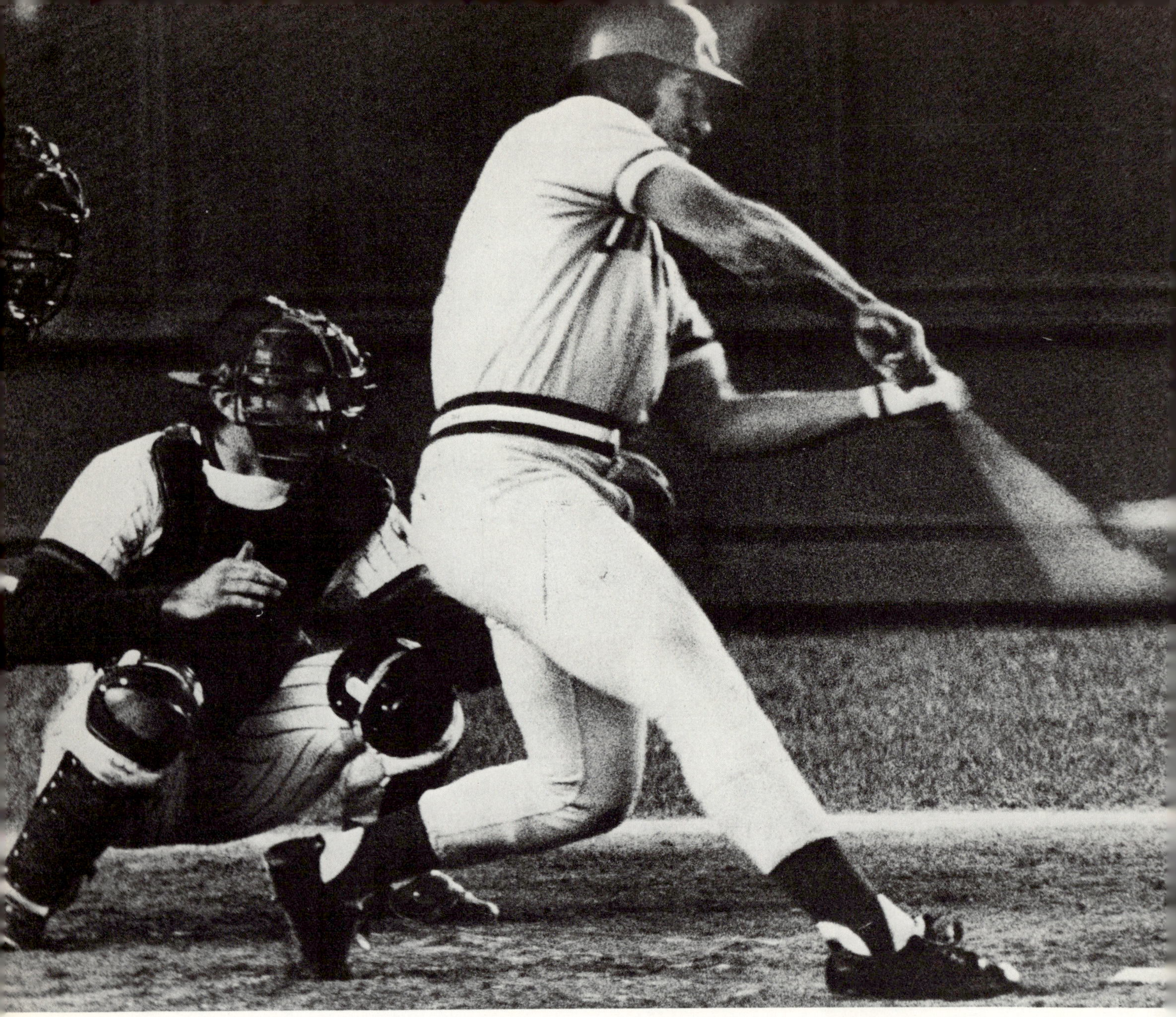

New York pitcher Craig Swan said I hit a good pitch, down and away.
As you can see, that's what I did, driving a single to left to set the
modern record, 38 straight games in the National League. It came in the
third inning of the July 25th game and I got two hits after that. I wanted
to keep after my 200-hit goal. Teams kept trying to pitch me away and
play me away. I just kept hitting it where they pitched it. That's always
my style.

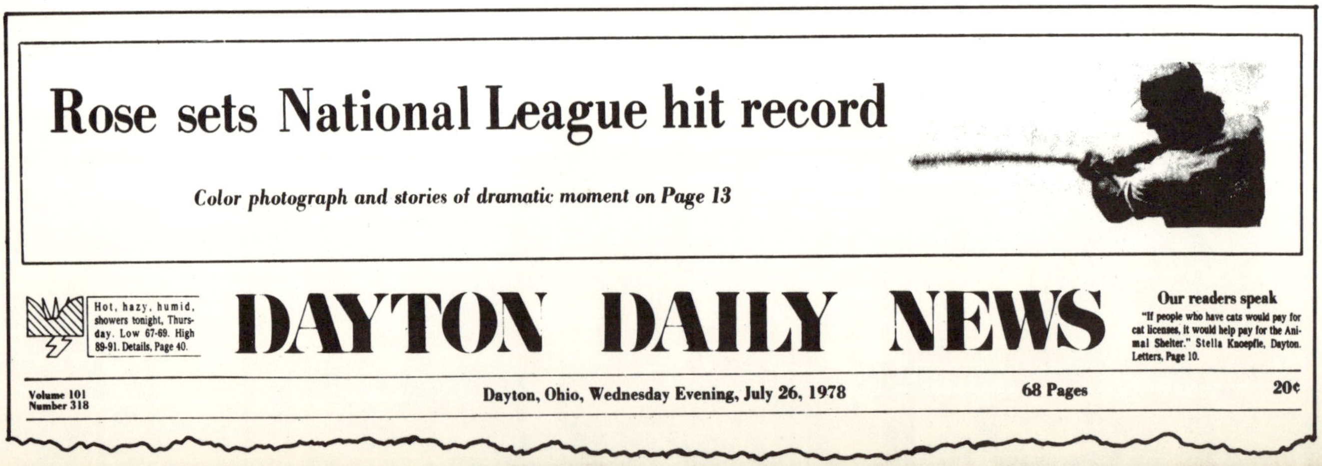

# Rose sets National League hit record

*Color photograph and stories of dramatic moment on Page 13*

# DAYTON DAILY NEWS



Volume 101
Number 318
Dayton, Ohio, Wednesday Evening, July 26, 1978
68 Pages
20¢

After breaking Tommy Holmes' record by singling in game 38, he ran on the field to congratulate me. I guess New York first baseman Willie Montanez was more flustered than I was. He kept trying to give me the ball to present to Holmes when he was supposed to give it to Holmes to present to me. I said, "Willie, give the ball to Tommy to give to me. I ain't gonna give it to Tommy. I hit the damn thing."

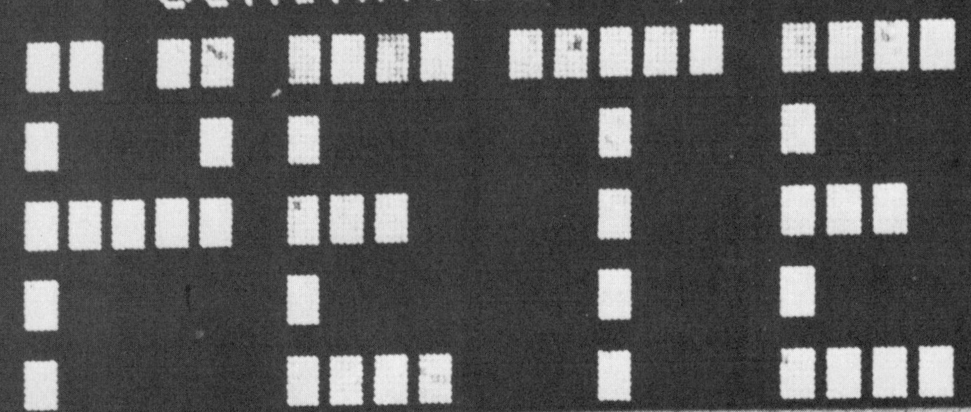

38 STRAIGHT GAMES
A NEW NATIONAL LEAGUE RECORD
CONGRATULATIONS

AT BAT 30    BALL 1    STRIKE 1    OUT 0
1 2 3 4 5 6 7 8 9 10   R   H   E
CIN. REDS   0 0         0   3   0
N.Y. METS   0 0         0   2   0
TOMORROW--REDS VS. METS 2 P.M.
Schaefer
Coke
CINCINNATI
14

◄ More class was shown me around the league than I believed
possible. Notice the scoreboard congratulating me for breaking
the record. I'm the enemy but the Mets are congratulating me.
Of course, there were 44,210 fans there and they sold something
like 18,000 at the gate. The Mets should have been happy about
the streak, right? I was more than happy to accommodate
everybody by getting base hits.

Newspapers had a lot of fun with my name during my streak. I
particularly liked this one in the New York Daily News after I set the
modern National League record with my 38th game: MIGHTY LIKE A
ROSE: 38. There was another one I liked: A ROSE BY ANY OTHER
NAME ISN'T PETE.

I won't be able to catch Ty Cobb's all-time hits record, 4,191, because he played in the big leagues 24 years. Though I'd like to, I don't think I'll make 24. I'm 37, with 16 years behind me, so I didn't do too badly. At least, I passed his best streaks, 40 in 1911 and 35 in 1917. My goal this year was to wipe out another Cobb record. We both had nine 200-hit seasons when 1978 started. I'm told Cobb and I were a lot alike—that we both lived for base hits, played as hard as we could, and ran the bases with abandon. I'm proud to be mentioned with a legend like Cobb.

George Sisler's son, Dick Sisler, was my manager in 1965 with the Reds.
If George was like Dick, he must have been a nice man. I led the league
in hits (209) and at bats (670) that year. Dick put my name in the lineup
every day, and I've been there ever since. I passed two of George
Sisler's streaks, 34 in 1925 and 41 in 1922, both made with the St. Louis
Browns.

**Wee Willie Keeler was the man I really wanted to catch after passing Tommy Holmes in game 38 for the modern National League record. Keeler hit in 44 straight in 1897 for Baltimore, three years before the modern era, so he is not officially recognized by baseball. But I didn't want anybody to say, "Well, Rose doesn't really have the all-time record, Keeler does." They tell me when Keeler did it, foul balls didn't count as strikes. I wish I had that advantage. Notice that Keeler is bunting. I bunted six times during my streak, four times when the bunts were my only hits. Wonder how many times Keeler bunted during his streak?**

"If you call making perfect bunts luck, well, it's not," Rose said. "Bunting takes a lot of work and practice. All through the streak, I haven't been lucky once. No generous scoring decisions, no close plays…nothing. I never got a checked-swing hit, never got one off a fielder's glove. They were all line drives, with a few perfect bunts mixed in. Those two bunts at Schmidt were perfect."

A new controversy swirled after that game. Some old-schoolers said Wee Willie Keeler of the old 1897 Baltimore Orioles held the real National League record, 44 straight, even though foul balls were not strikes. His record isn't recognized by baseball because only post-1900 records are considered the "modern era."

"I want to pass Keeler," Rose said. "The man must have been a helluva player and he couldn't help it if he was born before or after 1900. To me, he holds the National League record and I'm second…and second place don't cut it with me. I don't know much about Keeler, but he doesn't know much about me, either. I just know one thing. I'd like to go on hitting forever."

When he reached 42 on Saturday, July 29, with hits his first three times off Philadelphia's Jim Lonborg and Jim Kaat, Rose passed George Sisler and tied an ancient National Leaguer, Bill Dahlen. No. 43 was a line single to left in the fifth off Larry Christenson…a hit that didn't tie or pass anybody on the all-time lists. Ahead were Keeler's 44 and DiMaggio's 56. And, Sidney Stonestreet. Who?

"If I get Keeler, I'm going after Sidney Stonestreet," said Rose. "Sidney had 48. I invented him. I need a closer goal than 56."

The Courier-Journal, Sunday, July 30, 1978

# sports

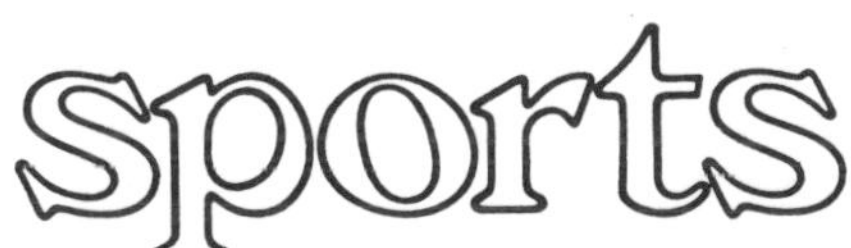

racing results • sports beat • outdoors

For major sports results, call 582-4871 ★

## *Summer of 42: Streaking Rose keeps up heat*

During my 44-game hitting streak, they announced in Cincinnati that The Phil Donahue Show was coming to town to tape a show with me. It was to be held in a small studio. But WLWT was staggered by 36,000 ticket requests. The entire 352 telephone exchange in Cincinnati was wiped out for the day. So they moved the show to the Riverfront Coliseum, an arena next to Riverfront Stadium and 6,000 people were there. Donahue is a good friend and a Reds' fan from the days when his show originated in Dayton, before he moved to Chicago. I enjoy doing TV shows. I did one other show with Donahue a few years back in the University of Dayton Arena in conjunction with a tennis tournament. Bobby Riggs and I were on and there were 5,000 for that show. Donahue said my two appearances had the first and second largest audiences his shows have had.

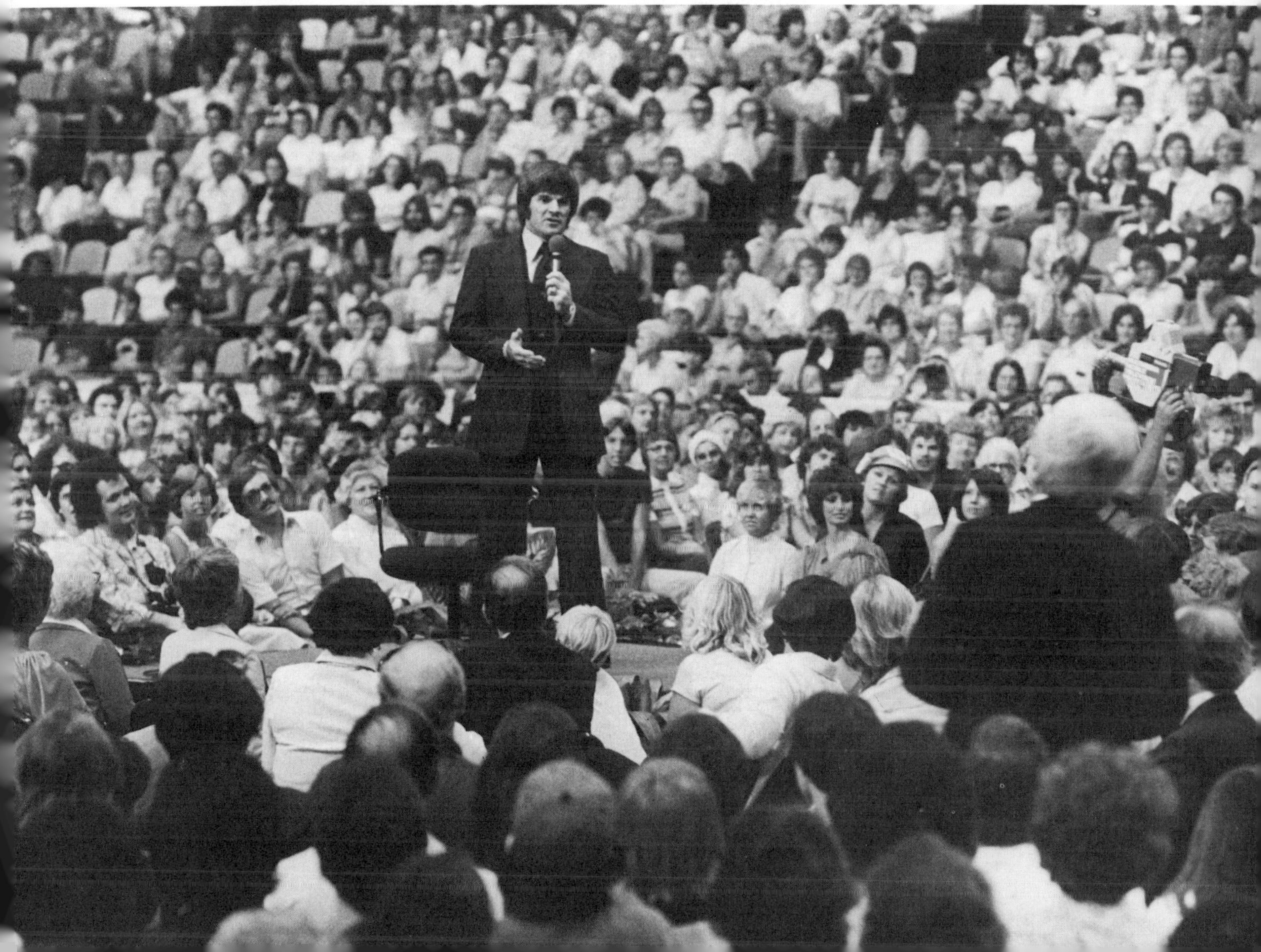

The Reds were heading for Atlanta and a three-game series the next day. Monday's pitcher was knuckleballer Phil Niekro, who called Rose in Cincinnati Sunday, asking him to appear with Niekro on his pre-game show. "Only if you throw me fastballs," Rose said. "No deal," Niekro answered.

"Well, I got a hit off your brother, Joe, against Houston, so I might as well keep it in the family."

With a season-high 45,007 in Atlanta Stadium cheering him on, Rose faced Niekro in the sixth, working the count to 2-and-0 on knucklers. Then came the fastball Rose was searching for, though Niekro said later it was a slider that didn't slide, and Pete pumped a ground single to right under diving second baseman Rod Gilbreath's glove...44 straight, move over Wee Willie.

Even Niekro shook Rose's hand, saying, "Pete is doing the greatest thing for baseball since the invention of the protective batting helmet. I would have liked to sit down on the mound and chat with Pete right then, but that would be heretical. After he got the hit, I was glad he got it. As a pitcher, maybe I shouldn't say it, but when you look up and see 45,000 people going crazy, it gives you a good feeling about the game. I walked him in the first inning and my own fans booed me. I never thought I'd be booed in Atlanta."

**There it comes, the pitch I hit under second baseman Rod Gilbreath's glove for the sixth-inning single that tied Wee Willie Keeler's all-time National League record of 44. Atlanta pitcher Phil Niekro said it was a slider, but it must not have broke. I thought it was a fast ball. Anyway, notice how I'm choking the bat. Makes it feel lighter. I'm getting old, you know.**

The New York Times
SPORTS
Rose Hits in 44th
And Ties Keeler


THE ATLANTA CONSTITUTION
Sports
Rose Hits Niekro To


Rose hits in 44th; Phillies win — Page 1-D
Philadelphia Inquirer
Tuesday, August 1, 1978

Every time I came up in Atlanta, the scoreboard spelled out "Pete" with big electronic X's. This is right after I tied Wee Willie Keeler's 44-game streak. Second baseman Rod Gilbreath is acting disgusted because the ball went right under his glove as he dove for it, one of the few ground ball singles during the streak. First base coach Ron Plaza is on his way to congratulate me.

So, Rose was level with Keeler at 44. DiMaggio was 12 games ahead.

The dreaded nemesis, a rookie pitcher, was in Rose's way on Tuesday, the first day of August. Larry McWilliams was starting his fourth major league game. And, he, too, like Niekro, was booed when he walked Rose to lead off the game.

Rose batted again in the second and drove a bolt through the box that the lanky left-handed pitcher deftly speared. In the fifth, Rose grounded to short. In the seventh, against reliever Gene Garber, he drove a liner that rookie third baseman Bob Horner picked off his navel.

Then came the dramatic ninth, the fans on their feet screaming, and Garber's piercing streak-ending strikeout, on a pitch that enraged Rose.

"The guy pitched me like it was the seventh game of the World Series," Rose snapped. "Hell, he was leading, 16-4. What's he doing throwing me three changeups on one at-bat? I hope I face him tomorrow in a close game. I want to drive one at him right through the box...and I mean hard."

**I was facing a 24-year-old rookie left-hander, Larry McWilliams.**

There has to be a villain, and Gene Garber is it. He's about to throw me the pitch that ended it all.

The crowd wouldn't leave until Rose was retrieved from the clubhouse for a final bow. In the post-game interview room, Rose said, "If third baseman Horner hadn't caught my ball, they'da had to take him to the hospital to dig it out. I'm not relieved that the streak is over, I'm pissed off. I really wanted to catch DiMag.

"I don't know how McWilliams caugh my liner, I swear to God I don't," he said. For 20 minutes, McWilliams sat silently next to Rose at the interview table and Rose didn't recognize him. Finally, a writer asked, "Would you know McWilliams if he were sitting next to you?"

"No," said Rose.

"Well, meet Larry McWilliams."

Rose slammed his fist on the table and said, "Damn, kid. Why did you catch that ball? They aren't gonna like you in Cincinnati."

**I've just missed the third strike. Catcher Joe Nolan is as happy as I am sad.**

You might call this the only encore of my career. After I struck out to end the streak, I went to the clubhouse and tore off my uniform top quickly. Equipment manager Bernie Stowe came running in and said, "You gotta go back out there. Nobody is leaving and they're all standing and yelling your name." So I went back out and waved. I got goose pimples. Those fans were paying me one helluva compliment—Atlanta fans. I would have liked to have gone in the stands to shake each one's hand. Thank you, Atlanta baseball fans, I'll never forget what you did.

They like Pete in Cincinnati, though…they love him, they adore him, even though Joe Morgan says that craggy face is one that only Aqua Velva could love.

Fans were genuinely worried about the 37-year-old Rose's future in Cincinnati. His contract expired after the 1978 season after a two-year run of $465,000 in 1977 and $265,000 in 1978, the $200,000 in difference coming from a bonus he received for signing in 1977.

For some reason, Rose and the Reds are always at odds at the bargaining table. "I just hope I don't start World War III over it," Rose said.

Whatever he gets, he deserves every nickel—if for no other reason than the fans he stuffed into the parks during the most exciting month and a half in recent baseball history.

**This rookie, Larry McWilliams, is sitting quietly next to me in the interview room and I didn't even realize it. He'll go down in history in a better way than the guy who threw Roger Maris his 61st homer the year he broke the Babe's record. Too bad McWilliams—or Gene Garber— wasn't my Tracy Stallard.**

**The New York Times**

NESDAY, AUGUST 2, 1978

Rose's Streak Ended at 44 as He G

# Sports

SECTION D

★★★ Wednesday, August 2, 1978

# Streak Ends

CINCINNATI ENQUIRE

**Braves Stop Rose's Streak At 44 Gam**

## Summing Up
## The Streak

- Batted .385 on 70-for-182
- Batted .397 against righthanded pitchers (46-for-116)
- Batted .364 against lefthanded pitchers (24-for-66)
- Had eleven 2-hit games; six 3-hit games; one 4-hit game
- Hit safely in the first inning 15 times
- Extended the streak with a hit in his final at bat six times
- Had 14 doubles, no triples, no homers; scored 30 runs, had 11 RBIs
- Walked 12 times and struck out five times
- Had six bunt hits, four of which were his only hit in the game

For sure, it will be a sad day in my life when I make that last lonely walk as a player up the narrow tunnel from the dugout to the clubhouse. I've made that walk for 16 years now, and I'll miss it. I'll miss the dugout, I'll miss the clubhouse. I'll miss the fans, my teammates, my opponents, the writers and broadcasters, everyone and everything connected with baseball. And after I make the last walk, I hope they see fit to honor me with acceptance into the Hall of Fame, so I can share my memories with the fans of the future.

# Pete's Streak, Game by Game

| Date, Opponent, Pitchers | AB | R | H | 2B* | RBI |
|---|---|---|---|---|---|
| 1—June 14, Chicago, Roberts | 4 | 1 | 2 | 0 | 0 |
| 2—June 16, St. Louis, Denny | 4 | 1 | 2 | 1 | 2 |
| 3—June 17, St. Louis, Vuckovich, Schultz | 4 | 2 | 2 | 0 | 0 |
| 4—June 18, St. Louis, S. Martinez | 4 | 1 | 1 | 0 | 0 |
| 5—June 20, San Francisco, Montefusco | 5 | 2 | 2 | 1 | 0 |
| 6—June 21, San Francisco, Halicki | 4 | 0 | 1 | 0 | 0 |
| 7—June 22, San Francisco, Knepper | 4 | 0 | 1 | 0 | 0 |
| 8—June 23, Los Angeles, Hooton | 4 | 0 | 1 | 0 | 0 |
| 9—June 24, Los Angeles, Welch | 5 | 1 | 4 | 1 | 0 |
| 10—June 25, Los Angeles, John | 3 | 1 | 2 | 0 | 0 |
| 11—June 26, Houston, Lemongello | 5 | 1 | 1 | 0 | 0 |
| 12—June 27, Houston, J. Niekro | 4 | 1 | 1 | 0 | 1 |
| 13—June 28, Houston, Dixon | 4 | 0 | 1 | 0 | 0 |
| 14—June 29, Houston, Bannister | 3 | 0 | 1 | 1 | 0 |
| 15—June 30, Los Angeles, Rautzhan | 4 | 1 | 1 | 0 | 0 |
| 16—June 30, Los Angeles, Welch, Forster, Hough | 5 | 1 | 3 | 0 | 0 |
| 17—July 1, Los Angeles, Rhoden | 5 | 0 | 1 | 1 | 0 |
| 18—July 2, Los Angeles, Rau | 4 | 1 | 1 | 1 | 0 |
| 19—July 3, Houston, Bannister, McLaughlin | 5 | 1 | 3 | 1 | 1 |
| 20—July 4, Houston, Richard | 4 | 1 | 1 | 0 | 0 |
| 21—July 5, Houston, J. Niekro | 4 | 0 | 1 | 0 | 0 |
| 22—July 7, San Francisco, Blue, Curtis | 5 | 1 | 3 | 0 | 1 |
| 23—July 7, San Francisco, Barr | 4 | 0 | 1 | 0 | 0 |
| 24—July 8, San Francisco, Montefusco | 4 | 1 | 1 | 0 | 0 |
| 25—July 9, San Francisco, Halicki, Knepper | 4 | 1 | 3 | 0 | 1 |
| 26—July 13, New York, Koosman, Lockwood | 5 | 0 | 2 | 1 | 1 |
| 27—July 14, New York, Zachry | 5 | 0 | 2 | 0 | 1 |
| 28—July 15, New York, Swan | 2 | 2 | 1 | 0 | 0 |
| 29—July 16, New York, Seibert | 5 | 1 | 1 | 1 | 0 |
| 30—July 17, Montreal, Bahnsen | 4 | 0 | 1 | 0 | 0 |
| 31—July 18, Montreal, Dues | 4 | 0 | 2 | 1 | 0 |
| 32—July 19, Philadelphia, Reed | 4 | 1 | 1 | 0 | 0 |
| 33—July 20, Philadelphia, Kaat | 5 | 1 | 1 | 0 | 0 |
| 34—July 21, Montreal, Grimsley | 3 | 1 | 1 | 0 | 1 |
| 35—July 22, Montreal, Schatzeder | 3 | 0 | 1 | 0 | 1 |
| 36—July 23, Montreal, Rogers, Knowles | 6 | 0 | 2 | 1 | 1 |
| 37—July 24, New York, Zachry, Lockwood | 5 | 2 | 2 | 0 | 0 |
| 38—July 25, New York, Swan | 4 | 1 | 3 | 1 | 0 |
| 39—July 26, New York, Espinosa | 3 | 0 | 1 | 1 | 0 |
| 40—July 28, Philadelphia, Lerch | 2 | 1 | 1 | 1 | 0 |
| 41—July 28, Philadelphia, Carlton | 4 | 0 | 1 | 0 | 0 |
| 42—July 29, Philadelphia, Lonborg, Kaat | 4 | 1 | 3 | 0 | 0 |
| 43—July 30, Philadelphia, Christenson, Reed | 5 | 0 | 2 | 0 | 0 |
| 44—July 31, Atlanta, P. Niekro | 4 | 0 | 1 | 0 | 0 |
| Aug. 1, Atlanta, McWilliams, Garber | 4 | 1 | 0 | 0 | 0 |
| **Totals** | **186** | **31** | **70** | **14** | **11** |

*No triples or home runs hit during streak.

# Baseball's Longest Hitting Streaks

| Name | Year | Games | Name | Year | Games |
|---|---|---|---|---|---|
| Joe DiMaggio (AL) | 1941 | 56 | John Stone (AL) | 1930 | 34 |
| Willie Keeler (NL) | 1897 | 44 | George Davis (NL) | 1893 | 33 |
| Pete Rose (NL) | 1978 | 44 | Rogers Hornsby (NL) | 1922 | 33 |
| Bill Dahlen (NL) | 1894 | 42 | Heinie Manush (AL) | 1933 | 33 |
| George Sisler (AL) | 1922 | 41 | Rico Carty (NL) | 1970 | 31 |
| Ty Cobb (AL) | 1911 | 40 | Fred Clarke (NL) | 1895 | 31 |
| Tommy Holmes (NL) | 1945 | 37 | Willie Davis (NL) | 1969 | 31 |
| Billy Hamilton (NL) | 1894 | 36 | Sam Rice (AL) | 1924 | 31 |
| Ty Cobb (AL) | 1917 | 35 | Goose Goslin (AL) | 1934 | 30 |
| Dom DiMaggio (AL) | 1949 | 34 | Ron LeFlore (AL) | 1976 | 30 |
| George McQuinn (AL) | 1938 | 34 | Stan Musial (NL) | 1950 | 30 |
| George Sisler (AL) | 1925 | 34 | Elmer Smith (NL) | 1898 | 30 |

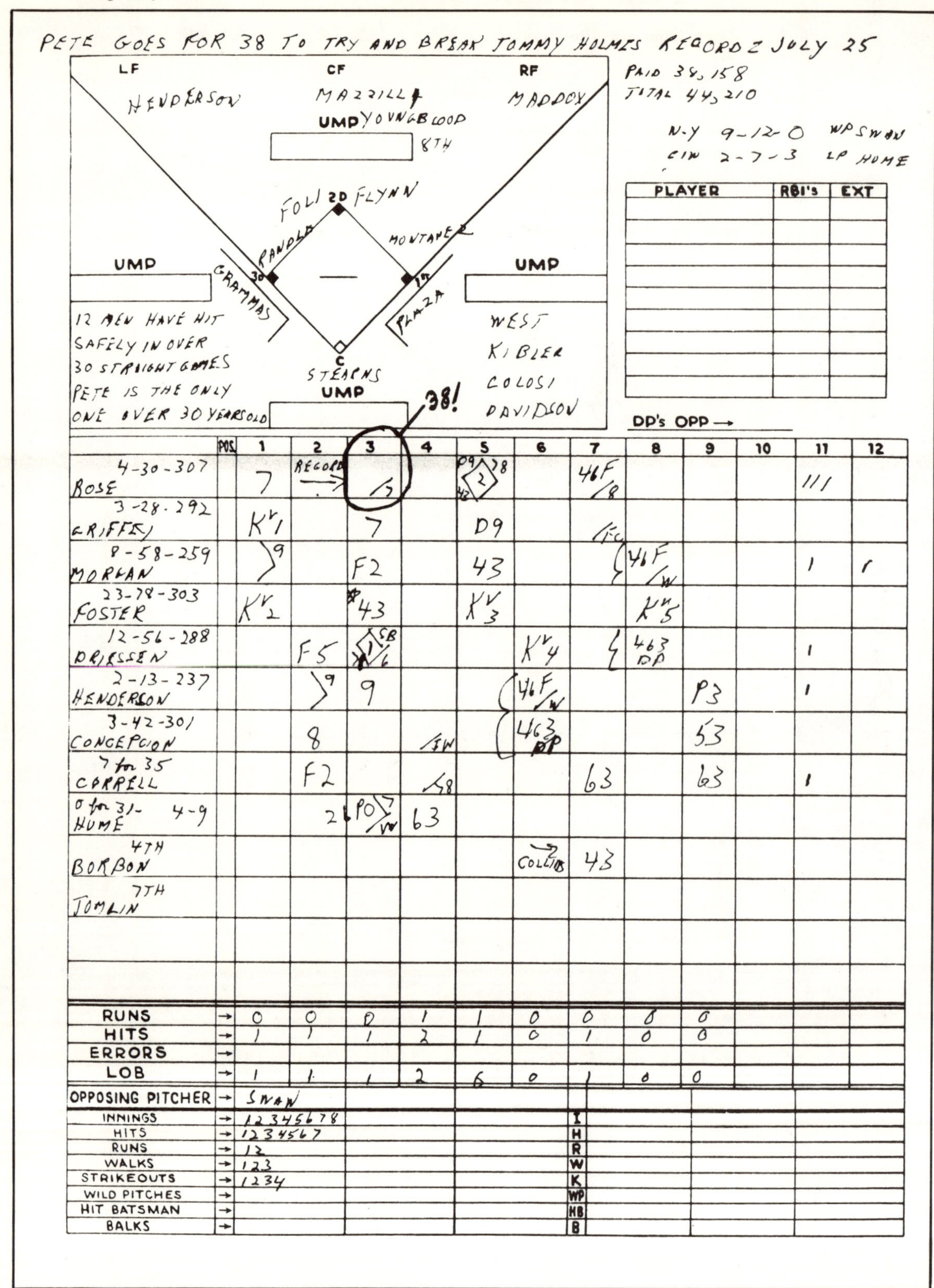



| PLAYER | RBI's | EXT |
|--------|-------|-----|
|  |  |  |
|  |  |  |
|  |  |  |
|  |  |  |
|  |  |  |
|  |  |  |
|  |  |  |

DP's OPP →

| | POS | 1 | 2 | 3 | 4 | 5 | 6 | 7 | 8 | 9 | 10 | 11 | 12 |
|---|---|---|---|---|---|---|---|---|---|---|---|---|---|
| 4-30-.307 ROSE | | 7 | RECORD | 7 | D9 28 | 46F/8 | | | | | | 111 | |
| 3-28-.292 GRIFFEY | | K¹ | | 7 | D9 | | (Fc | | | | | | |
| 8-58-.259 MORGAN | | 9 | F2 | | 43 | | 46F/W | | | 1 | | | 1 |
| 23-78-.303 FOSTER | | K²ᵛ | 43 | | K³ᵛ | | Kᴴ5 | | | | | | |
| 12-56-.288 DRIESSEN | | F5 | 1/6 SB | | Kᵛ4 | | 463 DP | | | | 1 | | |
| 2-13-.237 HENDERSON | | 9 | 9 | | 46F/W | | | P3 | | | 1 | | |
| 3-42-.301 CONCEPCION | | 8 | | 3W | 463 DP | | | 53 | | | | | |
| 7 for 35 CARRELL | | F2 | | 8 | | 63 | | 63 | | 1 | | | |
| 0 for 31- 4-9 HUME | | 2 PO/W | 63 | | | | | | | | | | |
| 4TH BORBON | | | | | | COLLIN 43 | | | | | | | |
| 7TH TOMLIN | | | | | | | | | | | | | |
| | | | | | | | | | | | | | |
| RUNS → | | 0 | 0 | 0 | 1 | 1 | 0 | 0 | 0 | 0 | | | |
| HITS → | | 1 | 1 | 1 | 2 | 1 | 0 | 1 | 0 | 0 | | | |
| ERRORS → | | | | | | | | | | | | | |
| LOB → | | 1 | 1 | 1 | 2 | 6 | 0 | 1 | 0 | 0 | | | |
| OPPOSING PITCHER → | SWAN | | | | | | | | | | | | |

| | | | | |
|---|---|---|---|---|
| INNINGS → | 12345678 | | I | |
| HITS → | 1234567 | | H | |
| RUNS → | 12 | | R | |
| WALKS → | 123 | | W | |
| STRIKEOUTS → | 1234 | | K | |
| WILD PITCHES → | | | WP | |
| HIT BATSMAN → | | | HB | |
| BALKS → | | | B | |

**This is Ken Coleman's scorecard for the Reds on the night Pete Rose broke Tommy Holmes' record by hitting in his 38th consecutive game. Coleman is one of Cincinnati's telecasters and he did the game at Shea Stadium in New York.**

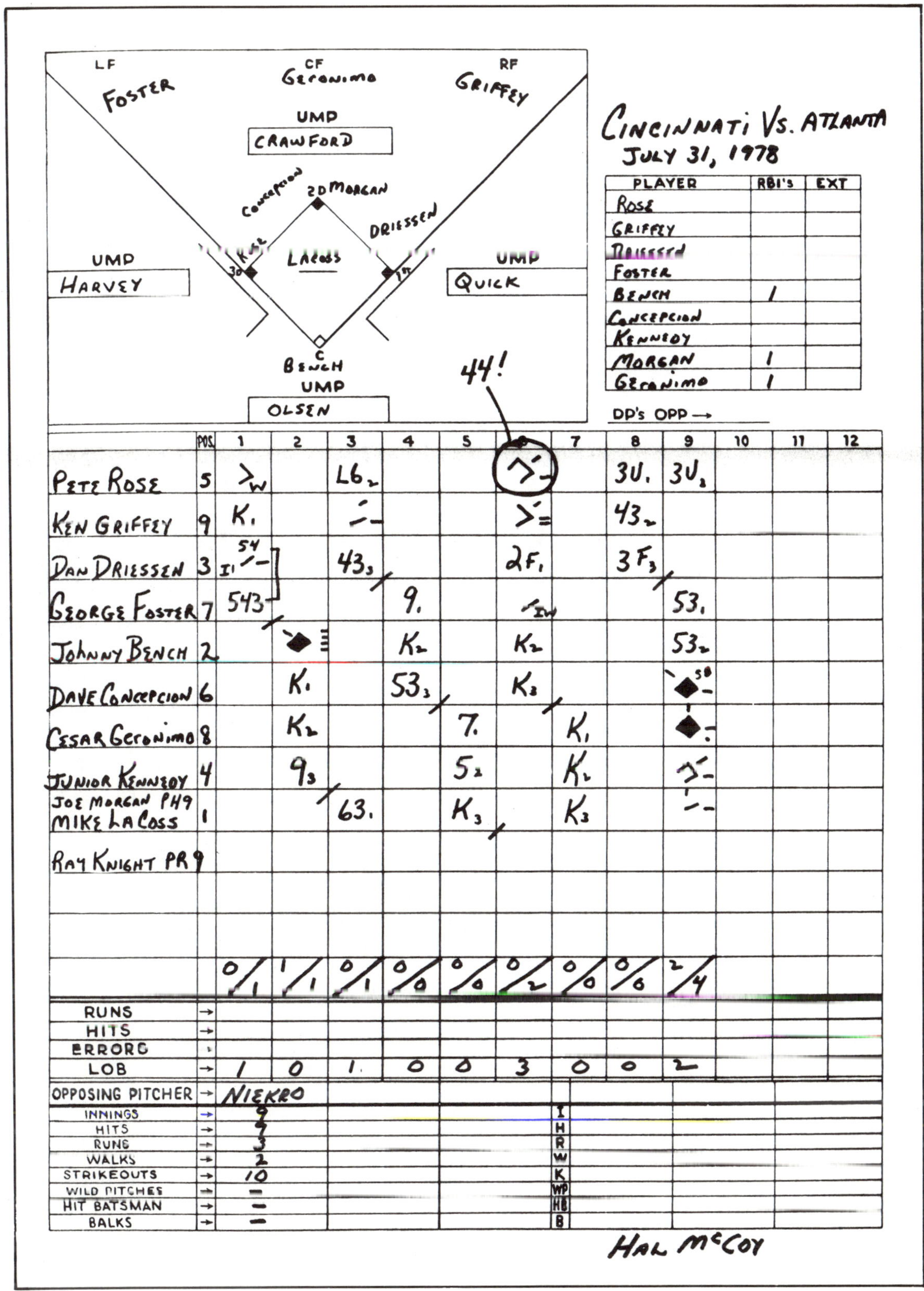


| PLAYER | RBI's | EXT |
|---|---|---|
| Rose | | |
| Griffey | | |
| Driessen | | |
| Foster | | |
| Bench | 1 | |
| Concepcion | | |
| Kennedy | | |
| Morgan | 1 | |
| Geronimo | 1 | |

DP's OPP →

| | POS | 1 | 2 | 3 | 4 | 5 | 6 | 7 | 8 | 9 | 10 | 11 | 12 |
|---|---|---|---|---|---|---|---|---|---|---|---|---|---|
| Pete Rose | 5 | ⟩W | | L6₂ | | | ⟨ | | 3U. | 3U₂ | | | |
| Ken Griffey | 9 | K₁ | | ·- | | | ⟩= | | 43₂ | | | | |
| Dan Driessen | 3 | I¹ 54 | | 43₃ | | | 2F₁ | | 3F₃ | | | | |
| George Foster | 7 | 543 | | | 9. | | ᵢₙ | | | 53₁ | | | |
| Johnny Bench | 2 | | ◆ | | K₂ | | K₂ | | | 53₂ | | | |
| Dave Concepcion | 6 | | K₁ | 53₃ | | | K₃ | | | ◆ 58 | | | |
| Cesar Geronimo | 8 | | K₂ | | 7. | | K₁ | | ◆ | | | | |
| Junior Kennedy | 4 | | 9₃ | | 5₂ | | K₂ | | | ⟩- | | | |
| Joe Morgan PH9 / Mike LaCoss | 1 | | | 63. | K₃ | | K₃ | | | ·- | | | |
| Ray Knight PR9 | | | | | | | | | | | | | |
| | | 0/1 | 1/1 | 0/1 | 0/0 | 0/0 | 0/2 | 0/0 | 0/6 | 2/4 | | | |

| | | 1 | 2 | 3 | 4 | 5 | 6 | 7 | 8 | 9 | 10 | 11 | 12 |
|---|---|---|---|---|---|---|---|---|---|---|---|---|---|
| RUNS | → | | | | | | | | | | | | |
| HITS | → | | | | | | | | | | | | |
| ERRORS | | | | | | | | | | | | | |
| LOB | → | 1 | 0 | 1. | 0 | 0 | 3 | 0 | 0 | 2 | | | |

| OPPOSING PITCHER | → | NIEKRO | | | | | | | |
|---|---|---|---|---|---|---|---|---|---|
| INNINGS | → | 9 | | | | I | | | |
| HITS | → | 9 | | | | H | | | |
| RUNS | → | 3 | | | | R | | | |
| WALKS | → | 2 | | | | W | | | |
| STRIKEOUTS | → | 10 | | | | K | | | |
| WILD PITCHES | → | — | | | | WP | | | |
| HIT BATSMAN | → | — | | | | HB | | | |
| BALKS | → | — | | | | B | | | |



This is Hal McCoy's scorecard for the Reds on the night Pete Rose hit in his 44th straight game to tie Wee Willie Keeler. Hal McCoy covered the game in Atlanta for the Dayton Daily News.

# CONGRATULATIONS

It's going to be a long winter for Helen Fabri. She, with the help of her husband Tony, answers my mail. I can't believe the amount of letters and telegrams I received as a result of the streak. There were thousands of them and they came from everywhere—as far away as Hong Kong. And what a lineup—Bill Cosby, Dom DiMaggio, Toni Tennille, Sidney Stonestreet's mother…

---

**western union**                    **Telegram**

```
        CTB177(1419)(4-028760E210)PD 07/29/78 1419
ICS IPMRNCZ CSP
 2138816538 TDRN LOS ANGELES CA 17 07-29 0219P EST
PMS PETE ROSE CINCINNATI REDS

CINCINNATI RIVER FRONT STADIUM, DLR
201 EAST 2ND ST
CINCINNATI OH
WHEN YOU GET THROUGH WITH JOE DIMAGGIO'S RECORD MY RECORD IS 84
STRAIGHT GAMES HEY HEY HEY
   FAT ALBERT
NNNN
```

**western union**                    **Telegram**

```
        AAA449(2303)(4-078599E213)PD 08/01/78 2302
ICS IPMMTZZ CSP
 6075478947 TDMT COOPERSTOWN NY 29 08-01 1102P EST
PMS PETE ROSE, AFTER 10AM, DLR
MARRIOTT HOTEL
ATLANTA GA
AT COOPERSTOWN AND EVERYWHERE PETE ROSE IS MOST EXCITING AND ADMIRED
 NAME IN USA. HALL OF FAME EAGER RECEIVE RECORD BAT WHEN FINISHED
 USING. ASKED STOVE HELP GRATEFULLY
   KEN SMITH HALL OF FAME
NNNN
```

```
CINCINNATI REDS

BASEBALL QFC
MR. PETE ROSE
% CINCINNATI REDS
100 RIVERFRONT STADIUM
CINCINNATI, OH 45202

DEAR PETE:

I'M SO DARNED PROUD OF YOU THAT FOR ONCE WORDS ALMOST FAIL ME.
I'M SURE EVERYONE IN BASEBALL FEELS THE SAME WAY.  THEY SHOULD.
YOU HAVE BROUGHT NOTHING BUT HONOR TO OUR GAME NOT ONLY BY YOUR
STREAK BUT MORE THAN ANYTHING ELSE BY JUST BEING PETE ROSE WITH
EVERYTHING THAT HAS STOOD FOR THE LAST SIXTEEN YEARS.

BEST REGARDS,

BOWIE KUHN
TKSM END
```

**western union** — **Telegram**

```
         CTA200(1418)(4-028705E210)PD 07/29/78 1418
ICS IPMRNCZ CSP
 2138816538 TDRN LOS ANGELES CA 13 07-29 0218P EST
PMS PETE ROSE CINCINNATI REDS

CINCINNATI RIVER FRONT STADIUM, DLR
201 EAST 2ND ST
CINCINNATI OH
LIKE I TOLD THE MAN AT THE BACCARET TABLE RUN OUT THE SHOE
  BILL COSBY
NNNN
```

**western union** — **Telegram**

```
       CTB298(1508)(1-017194A215)PD 08/03/78 1507
TWX NATLLEAGUE NYK
 1 DLY NEW YORK, NY - AUG. 3, 1978
PMS PETE ROSE
CINCINNATI REDS
100 RIVERFRONT STADIUM
CINCINNATI, OHIO 45202
NICE GOING.  ALL THE NATIONAL LEAGUE IS PROUD OF YOU.  SEE YOU SOON.
CHUB FEENEY
NNNN
```

**western union** — **Telegram**

```
       AAC158(1252)(1-017920C213)PD 08/01/78 1251
TWX WU CTRL BRID
801 BRIDGETON MO
PMS PETE ROSE
ATLANTA STADIUM
ATLANTA GA

ATTN CHARLES T NEWTON, PLS HAND DLR PERSONALLY

GO PETE GO....ALL THE WAY PAST JOLTIN JOE.....

ST LOUIS BROWNS FAN CLUB
```

    MIC318

 ZCZC MIC319 231014

IMA207 MBC109

MIX453 231003

CYA008(1002)(4-008091E204)PD 07/23/78 1002

ICS IPMMTZZ CSP

 6177480023 TDMT MARION MA 28 07-23 1002A EST

PMS PETE ROSE, CARE MONTREAL EXPOS OLYMPIC STADIUM

MONTREAL PQ CAN


BT

YOU HAVE JUST PASSED ME ON THE ALL TIME CONSECUTIVE GAME HITTING

 STREAK LIST. MY CONGRATULATIONS. MAY CONTINUED GOOD LUCK BE WITH YOU

 ON THE REST OF YOUR JOURNEY.

    DOM DIMAGGIO

---

    CINCINNATI REDS
    P
    CINCINNATI REDS

    CINCINNATI REDS

    WU INFOMASTER   1-034531C207 07/26/78
    ICS IPMCTOC CIN
     03132 (4-064652E207) 07-26 1900
    TWX 8104612097 CINCINNATI REDS
    ICS IPMMTZZ CSP
    7027347743 TDMT LAS VEGAS NV 61 07-26 0700P EST
    PETE ROSE
    CARE CINCINNATI REDS BASEBALL TEAM
    100 RIVERFRONT STADIUM
    CINCINNATI OH 45202
    DEAR PETE, HOORAY FOR THE ROSE. EVEN THOUGH I BLEED DODGER BLUE
    I'M SO HAPPY FOR YOU AND THE TERRIFIC EXAMPLE YOU SET FOR ALL OF US
    ON THE FAR SIDE OF 35. THE BEST YEARS ARE YET TO COME AND PETE ROSE
    SHOWS THE WAY. YOU ARE THE TRUE SPIRIT OF MAJOR LEAGUE BALL.
    KEEP ON SWINGING. PETE
       TONI TENNILE
    2052 EST

    CINCINNATI REDS

## Telegram

```
        CTB399(1734)(4-063144E209)PD 07/28/78 1733
ICS IPMMTZZ CSP
 2167342206 TDMT WESTLAKE OH 13 07-28 0533P EST
PMS PETE ROSE, DLR
RIVERFRONT STADIUM
CINCINNATI OH
PETE, CONGRATULATIONS ON YOUR GREAT ACHIEVEMENT. NO ONE IS MORE
DESERVING. CONTINUED SUCCESS
   AN OLD FOE RICK WISE
NNNN
```

## Telegram

```
       AAD170(1354)(4-040953E213)PD 08/01/78 1354
ICS IPMBNGZ CSP
 6062660075 TDBN LEXINGTON KY 20 08-01 0154P EST
PMS PETE ROSE, CARE CINCINNATI BASEBALL CLUB, DLR
ATLANTA STADIUM
ATLANTA GA
NOW ALL YOU NEED IS A LOUSY ONE IN EVERY FOUR IN A LITTLE OLD TWELVE
 GAME STREAK. BEST WISHES FROM SIDNEY WHOSE MAIL PRIVILEGES ARE
 BANNED THIS MONTH
   SIDNEY'S MOTHER
NNNN
```

## Telegram

```
       CTA398(1907)(4-06640SZ215)PD 08/03/78 1907
ICS IPMMTZZ CSP
 8138226937 TDMT ST PETERSBURG FL 2 08-03 0707P EST
PMS MR PETE ROSE, DLR
CINCINNATI BASEBALL CLUB RIVERFRONT STADIUM
CINCINNATI OH
FROM ALL OF US IN THE MINOR LEAGUES YOU ARE OUR MAN OF THE YEAR IN
1978 OR ANY OTHER YEAR WE ARE PROUD OF THE HITTING STREAK BUT
PROUDER OF YOU
   BOBBY BRAGAN
NNNN
```

# AT LARGE

You can see my hair has been getting longer and longer and I know you've heard about manager Sparky Anderson's no long hair, no sideburns, no mustaches and no beards rules. He's fairly lenient except the no mustache rule. I let my hair get pretty long during my 44-game hitting streak and I told him I'd get it cut after the streak ended. But he told me not to worry about my hair, just get the hits. I just change with the times. Everybody else has long hair, so why should I be different? Man, I was ugly with that short hair, wasn't I?

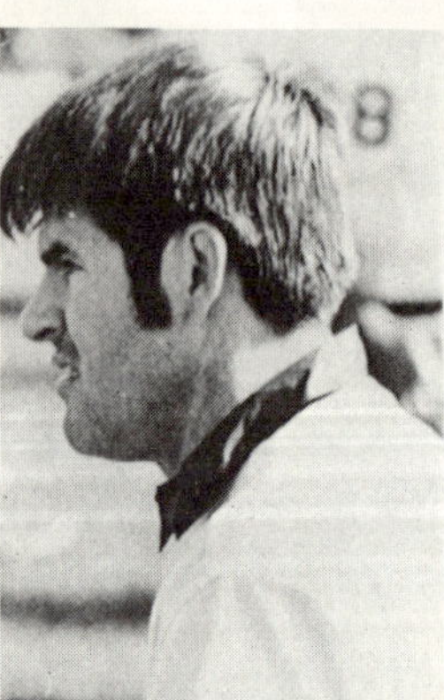

I'm in good company here with an ex-football player named Ford and Johnny Bench and Hank Aaron. It was Opening Day, 1974, and after the Atlanta Braves tried to keep Hank out of the lineup so he could go after home run No. 714 at home, Commissioner Bowie Kuhn stepped in and ordered the Braves to play Aaron in Riverfront. So he smashed No. 714 off Jack Billingham that day.

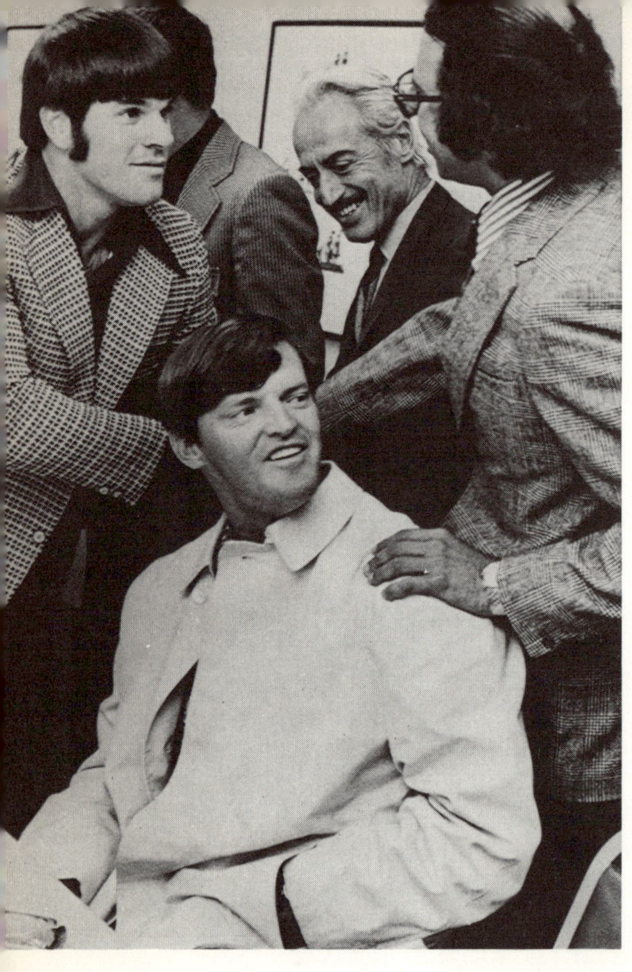

The Great Baseball Players Strike of 1972 cost us eight games. The strike continued beyond Opening Day and we never made up those eight games. It cost me a 200-hit season, which would have given me 10 going into 1978. I finished with 198, which still led the league. Relief pitcher Clay Carroll is the arm rest for player attorney Dick Moss, and player representative Marvin Miller is in the background. Yeah, it cost me 200 hits, but it did a lot of good for players as far as pension funds and benefits. You can't really second-guess what Marvin Miller has done; he has done a great job with the pension fund. That's why I'd never say much about missing the eight games or anything against the strike.

One of the super nice things about being a well-known athlete is the chance to meet famous athletes in all sports. That's Olympic distance champion Kip Keino with me, and I was as pleased to meet him as he was me. I was in Montreal at the Olympic Village in 1976 to help present 150 bicycles for village transportation to the International Olympic Committee.

I probably give as many autographs as anybody in baseball. But there's a time and a place for everything. A bad place to ask for an autograph is in a restaurant while a guy is trying to eat. If you give one, pretty soon there's a long line and before you know it, your pork chops are cold. I try to give autographs most of the time, but I don't like to stand before games reaching up, as I'm doing here in St. Petersburg during spring training. People like to get autographs at Cincinnati's Riverfront Stadium before a game, but the wall is so high that pretty soon your arms get tired. They don't make it convenient there. Old Crosley Field was convenient because the fences were low and you looked down at the people. At Riverfront, you reach up for 20 minutes and you're tired going into the game. I've had people knock on my hotel room door at 7:30 in the morning for an autograph and kids shove paper under my door to sign.

111

# WIDE WORLD
# OF SUPERSTARS

I was in the TV Superstars competition in 1974 and it was really fun, an off-beat thing that was nice because of the different people I met. I enjoyed it for a couple of reasons—and don't make any comments about my tennis form. I play tennis a lot in the off-season for its conditioning benefits. Manager Sparky Anderson doesn't allow tennis during the season. I played Bobby Riggs in an exhibition set in Dayton a few years back, too. The fun thing about the Superstars was meeting O.J. Simpson, Arthur Ashe, Stan Smith, Rod Laver—guys I don't normally see. They're all nice people. And it makes things easier when they've got to run the same obstacle course, as I'm doing here.

I'll never win a gold medal as a weightlifter. Or the Masters in golf. These were among the sports in the Superstars exhibition. Check out that golf swing. I don't even play golf and I had to have a birdie on 18 to beat out John Havlicek. I did it. I remember one hole where I hit the ball in the lake, but it skipped across and came out. The next shot went into the rough but bounced back to the fairway. I thought, "Man, you can't go wrong." My next shot went right into a sand trap. I had two breaks and still didn't do anything. Jack Nicklaus doesn't have to worry about me.

114

# ALL IN

Karolyn and I met at a horse race track and she insists she didn't know who I was, other than some kind of athlete. She thought I was a football player. She didn't know too much about baseball. She asked me what I did with all those bases I stole and I told her I put them in the trunk of my car. She believed me. We were married on a windy January day in 1964 at St. William's Church in Cincinnati. Her maiden name is Karolyn Ann Engelhardt.

# THE FAMILY

Our daughter Fawn is 13 now; this was taken at a somewhat earlier age in spring training.

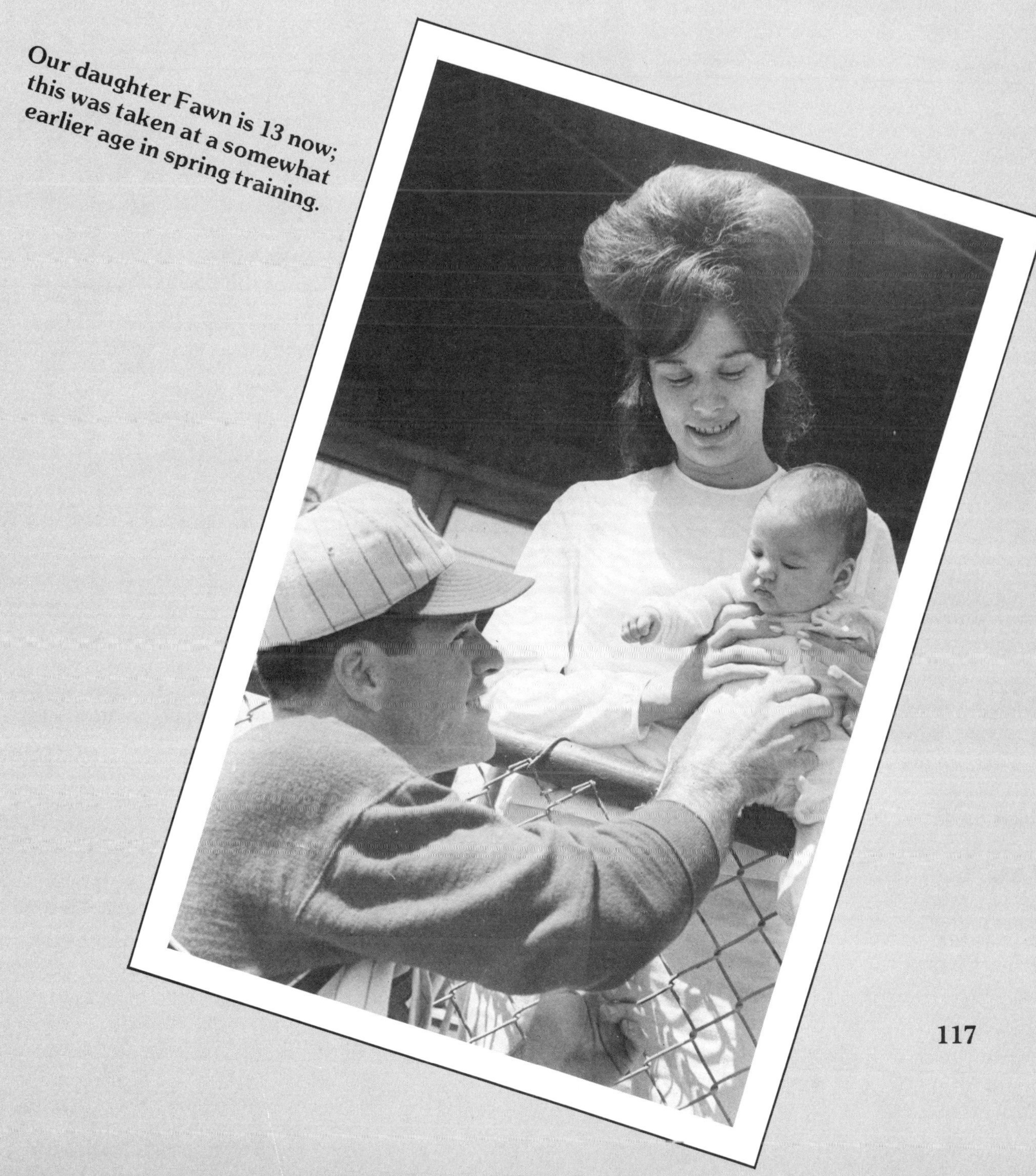

The baseball motif is around my home, as you might expect. My house actually is a lot bigger than it looks in the photo. Those seats around my swimming pool are from old Crosley Field in Cincinnati. I rescued them when they tore the old place down after Riverfront Stadium opened in 1970. Notice that baby picture above my fireplace? The guy who fixed that up said everything changed about me but my head.

Petie Jr., is eight and one helluva ballplayer already. He's a fighter, too, and I can't imagine where he gets it. The only problem with him, and I guess you have it with all little kids, is trying to get them to practice all the time, really work at it. There are just so many other things for them to do nowadays, things that weren't around to distract me when I was a kid. They lose their concentration so easily, and as a dad, I try to watch that. Concentration is probably my No. 1 asset. But, he has a uniform with Rose and 14 on it, just like mine. I took him to the All-Star Game in San Diego and the players were calling us 14-A and 14-B.

Doby, my Doberman Pinscher, is a big guy now, but he wasn't when Earl Lawson of the Cincinnati Post visited the house to do a story and Karolyn gave him a hot dog. Just as Earl was about to pop it into his mouth, Doby jumped on him and grabbed the hot dog. I don't even remember where I got him. We didn't train him to be an attack dog, but most people won't mess around a house where they know there's a Doberman around. You'd be surprised, even when friends come, they see Doby and they get scared.

We used to decorate houses with toilet paper on Halloween, but this was something else. When I got back after we won the 1975 World Series in Boston, my house resembled a billboard. Our neighbors covered it with signs, congratulating the Reds for winning the Series and me for winning the World Series MVP award.

120

I have a Halloween party at my house every year.
Now, I know you can pick me out in the picture
with the cannibal. That's Bob Connolly, owner of
Ohio Valley Wine Company, and he looks as if he's
dined on too many people. In the picture with two
other guys, that's me on the left with Peppe
Ramundo, my tailor, and Gordon Granick, owner
of the Cincinnati Shoe Company. No one knew me
with the costume on. I had oversized shoes, the
mask, everything covered. Do you think that mask
might scare Randy Jones?

PACER X

I don't really drive a Pacer. I drive a Rolls Royce and a Porsche. The Pacer was a promotional thing, for my winning the Sport MVP award in the 1975 World Series. They actually gave me a jeep. I always liked cars because I never had one as a kid. I got my first car when I graduated from high school and my mom bought me a 1937 Plymouth for $100. It didn't have a bumper on the front, but it had a stereo. I'm really proud of my Rolls and it reminds me of one of the funnier stories about cars. Clay Carroll, one of the all-time great relief pitchers for us in the early-1970's, was a down-home country boy from Alabama. He bought a Cadillac and Tommy Helms told him, "You driving a Cadillac is like putting earrings on a pig." Even Clay thought it was funny.

# CINCINNATI'S

I have two restaurants in Cincinnati. The newest is the Pete Rose Champion Restaurant. I spend as much time at one or the other as I can. I even eat there, so you know it must be good. I sit at a table and sign autographs or walk around talking to the customers. Karolyn even serves coffee sometimes. It's a fun business. I'm Cincinnati's Toots Shor. I'm overlooking the meat in the picture, but I don't cook. People Magazine took a picture of me cooking steaks on a grill, but I really wasn't. After they took the picture, I let the steaks burn.

124

# TOOTS SHOR

I used to have a real nice trophy room but all my big, special trophies
are in my new restaurant, about $35,000 to $40,000 worth out there. My
Hickok belt, valued at $15,000, is there, a silver bat (for winning the
batting title), some really prized mementos. They're all locked up, but
they make a great display. I don't know how much my entire collection
is worth. A lot of it is sentimental stuff—all the bats I used in All-Star
Games, all the 200-hit balls, the balls I hit for my 500th, 1,000th, 1,500th,
2,000th, 2,500th, 2,600th, 2,700th, 2,800th, 2,900th and 3,000th hits. I
have the ball I hit for my 1,882nd hit to pass Vada Pinson for the all-time
club lead. Any ball that means something, I keep it.

# PITCHING ON TV

Doing TV commercials is fun, brings out the ham in me. Probably my most famous one is the Aqua Velva commercial, where I got to sing, "There's something about an Aqua Velva man." A professional singer was supposed to sing the jingle and they were to dub it in over my voice. They rehearsed and rehearsed and rehearsed, but the guy couldn't get it the way they wanted. I said, "Like this, man," and belted it out. The TV people liked it so much they let me sing it myself. I like the one where I walk away with the female sportswriter. I did an underwear commercial for a national magazine and some woman on The Phil Donahue TV Show got on my case. I didn't think I looked so bad. Mine weren't as scanty as some of the others. I've also done ads for Zenith, Swanson Pizza and Mountain Dew, and now I'm selling my own brand of soda pop, a chocolate-flavored drink called—what else?—Pete.

# CINCINNATI REDS®

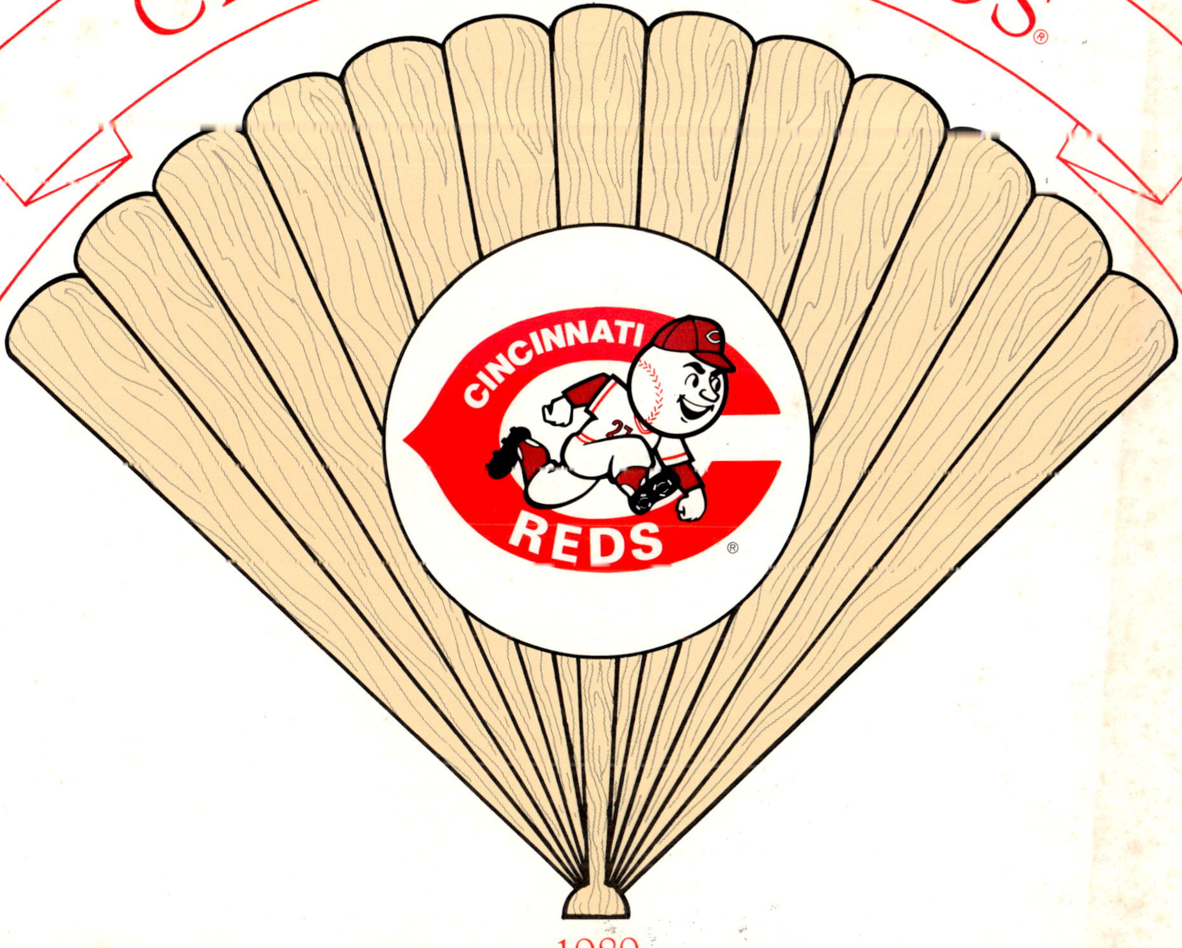

1989

50¢



S C O R E C A R D

# THE STRENGTH TO LEAD

## CUBS NUMERICAL ROSTER

2 Vance Law, INF
3 Jose Martinez, Coach
4 Don Zimmer, Manager
5 Chuck Cottier, Coach
6 Joe Altobelli, Coach
7 Joe Girardi, C
8 Andre Dawson, OF
9 Damon Berryhill, C
10 Lloyd McClendon, INF
12 Shawon Dunston, INF
15 Domingo Ramos, INF
17 Mark Grace, INF
18 Dwight Smith, OF
19 Curtis Wilkerson, INF
20 Jerome Walton, OF
21 Scott Sanderson, P
23 Ryne Sandberg, INF
28 Mitch Williams, P
30 Darrin Jackson, OF
31 Greg Maddux, P
32 Calvin Schiraldi, P
33 Mitch Webster, OF
34 Dick Pole, Coach
35 Larry Cox, Coach
36 Mike Bielecki, P
39 Paul Kilgus, P
40 Rick Sutcliffe, P
41 Jeff Pico, P
44 Steve Wilson, P
50 Les Lancaster, P

| CHICAGO | 1 | 2 | 3 | 4 | 5 | 6 | 7 | 8 | 9 | 10 | AB | R | H | RBI |
|---|---|---|---|---|---|---|---|---|---|---|---|---|---|---|
| | | | | | | | | | | | | | | |
| | | | | | | | | | | | | | | |
| | | | | | | | | | | | | | | |
| | | | | | | | | | | | | | | |
| | | | | | | | | | | | | | | |
| | | | | | | | | | | | | | | |
| | | | | | | | | | | | | | | |
| | | | | | | | | | | | | | | |
| | | | | | | | | | | | | | | |
| | | | | | | | | | | | | | | |
| | | | | | | | | | | | | | | |
| | | | | | | | | | | | | | | |
| | | | | | | | | | | | | | | |
| TOTALS | | | | | | | | | | | | | | |

# AN AMERICAN ARTIST IN AFRICA, 1937

## SKETCH BOOK and DIARY

## Wanda Norstrom

Foreword and Afterword by Georgiana Peacher

Pearl Shedding Press

*Cover art*: Actual size reproductions of water color, *Woman Cooking,* and *miniature* oil self portrait, by Wanda Norstrom.


Designed and Edited by Georgiana Peacher


Pearl Shedding Press
245 Broadway, 403
South Portland, Maine 04106